D1359258

The
NAZARENE

Forty Devotions on
the Lyrical Life of Jesus

MICHAEL CARD

An imprint of InterVarsity Press
Downers Grove, Illinois

InterVarsity Press
P.O. Box 1400, Downers Grove, IL 60515-1426
ivpress.com
email@ivpress.com

©2020 by Michael J. Card

All rights reserved. No part of this book may be reproduced in any form without written permission from
InterVarsity Press.

InterVarsity Press® is the book-publishing division of InterVarsity Christian Fellowship/USA®, a movement of students
and faculty active on campus at hundreds of universities, colleges, and schools of nursing in the United States of America,
and a member movement of the International Fellowship of Evangelical Students. For information about local and
regional activities, visit intervarsity.org.

All Scripture quotations, unless otherwise indicated, have been taken from the Christian Standard Bible®, Copyright
© 2017 by Holman Bible Publishers. Used by permission. Christian Standard Bible® and CSB® are federally registered
trademarks of Holman Bible Publishers.

While any stories in this book are true, some names and identifying information may have been changed to protect
the privacy of individuals.

Michael Card, Covenant Artists: song lyrics and music from Luke © 2011, Mark © 2012, Matthew © 2013,
John © 2014. Used by permission.

Cover design and image composite: Cindy Kiple
Interior design: Jeanna Wiggins
Images: clouds and water illustration © Pobytov / DigitalVision Vectors / Getty Images
   musical illustration © BEingNothing / DigitalVision Vectors / Getty Images

ISBN 978-0-8308-4801-0 (print)
ISBN 978-0-8308-4802-7 (digital)

Printed in the United States of America ∞

InterVarsity Press is committed to ecological stewardship and to the conservation of natural resources in all our operations.
This book was printed using sustainably sourced paper.

Library of Congress Cataloging-in-Publication Data
A catalog record for this book is available from the Library of Congress.

P 25 24 23 22 21 20 19 18 17 16 15 14 13 12 11 10 9 8 7 6 5 4 3 2 1
Y 37 36 35 34 33 32 31 30 29 28 27 26 25 24 23 22 21 20

To my children, Katie, Will, Nate,

and Maggie, and to my wife, Susan,

FOR FORTY YEARS OF OUR

OWN LYRICAL LIFE.

CONTENTS

PREFACE

BIBLICAL LYRICS:
Where Do They Come From?

PEOPLE SOMETIMES ASK, "What makes you want to write all those lyrics about the life of Jesus?" Depending on my frame of mind I answer that question different ways; people write songs about Jesus because they sense a burden to sing something meaningful to their own generation. They write because they've discovered some new facet of Jesus' life they have never heard anyone sing about. Sometimes I want to respond to that question with a question (which, by the way, is what Jesus often did!).

How can you *not* sing about him?

Like grief or joy, his lyrical life doesn't make complete sense until you set it to music, make the words rhyme, and fit the exacting structure of melody, meter, and poetry. From the very beginning that's what his followers did. His mother sang about it, as did Simeon, because for them the only way to adequately express it was to involve all of their being in resonating to the good news that he had come into the world. Paul borrowed a hymn in Philippians 2 in trying to come to grips with the mystery of the incarnation. The only way to make sense of the mystery was to sing; theologizing wasn't enough, is never enough.

Often, they come as a result of the desire the writer has for others to hear the message of Scripture, for truth is almost always sung before it's written down. (One of the best examples is the hymn to the incarnation in Philippians 2:6-11.) Lyrics come concentrated and condensed into three- or four-minute blocks, wrapped in a package of notes and carried along on a melody that should match the mood of the words like a hand in a glove. They should fit the story, the character. We should see a face when we hear the notes; we should be able to feel the emotions of the central subject. They should place the biblical character before our eyes, as if on a stage.

For me, personally, the final and conclusive answer to the question of where true biblical lyrics come from is this: they come from his life, the luminous life of the Light of the world, because in him all things have been created, even songs. The best of biblical songs come from engaging with the texts that present his life. As a result of listening to that life, to the sometimes scandalous things he would say, and even sometimes listening to the things he neglected to say, we find our hearts resonating with words and music. Listening to the responses of those who were immeasurably blessed to see him in the flesh, those who were drawn to, fascinated by, scandalized and repelled by him. Listening to his fragmented world, to the tiny pockets of quiet that seem to have been all too rare in his experience.

From all these layers of listening and more come truly biblical lyrics. They should be convicting but not coercive. They do not simply seek to superimpose the ideas of the writer onto the minds of the hearer but rather empower the hearer to think their own new thoughts and come to their own fresh conclusions, to make possible for the listener their own unique imaginative experience with the subject of the song.

HOW TO USE THIS BOOK

This book, and the recordings associated with it, are designed to be used in a number of different ways as determined by you. If you happen to be an auditory learner, perhaps you will find it helpful to listen to the songs first and then proceed to the essays in this book. If you are more verbal in your learning style, you might want to forgo listening to the songs and simply meditate on the lyrics before reading the essays. The devotions are deliberately brief to allow time to listen and read through the lyrics. The three parts are best experienced together in whatever order you choose.

Of the utmost importance is that you understand these lyrics are nothing more than an entrée to the biblical text they come from. No matter how you choose to engage with the lyrics, essays, and recorded material, the goal is that in the end you put them away and open your Bible.

1

The LYRICAL LIFE of the NAZARENE

The Nazarene had come to live
The life of everyman
And He felt the fascination
Of the stars
And as He wandered through this weary world
He wondered and He wept
For there were so few
Who'd listen to His call?
He came, He saw, He surrendered all
So that we might be born again
And the fact of His humanity
Was there for all to see
For He was unlike any other man
And yet so much like me
The Nazarene could hunger
And the Nazarene could cry
And He could laugh with all
The fullness of His heart
And those who hardly knew Him
And those who knew Him well
Could feel the contradiction
From the start

THE LYRICAL LIFE OF THE NAZARENE

If you listen, really listen, to the life of Jesus, you will hear a subtle resonance. Yes, it "rings true," but there is infinitely more to it than that. His life pulsates with an unspoken poetry; it vibrates in time with his life situation and those who found themselves within his reach. You might say his life was even a song in itself, or at least you could make a strong case for it being lyrical. It often rhymed beautifully. Sometimes it reverberated with a discord that in the end was still a meaningful resonance.

The lyricism and tone and color of the life of Jesus is one reason why so many of us write songs to him or paint pictures of him or seek to portray his remarkable life in any of a thousand other ways. In one sense, if you really listen, it is easy. There is so much depth. So many endlessly interesting scenes that no one could ever hope to squeeze dry. And in quite another sense, it is impossibly difficult because words fall so short and notes can only ring for a certain length of time. They are all clumsy bricks. Words can only resonate within their range of meaning. And melodies, even the vast soaring ones, are finite, limited to a key signature and a single time frame.

Nonetheless, easy or hard, we are left with his life. His beautiful, mysterious, frustrating, scandalous life. We are left with his words— comforting, challenging, enigmatic, dazzlingly, inescapably clear. His words resonate across time, through centuries. They fall on our listening ears and something pretuned in our hearts resonates with fresh melodies and lyrics, words and notes in honor of that lyrical life of his.

What follows is the result of a lifetime of fragmented attempts to listen to the lyrical life of the Nazarene. They are resonances I heard in my own heart and mind and shared along with the many cowriters whose names I will, with great gratitude, indicate. They were a result of trying to see Jesus' life from a different perspective, from a fresh point of view. Sometimes I almost got it right, more often I missed something vital. But even the songs that don't hit dead center are invitations for you to listen, maybe to listen better and more clearly, more biblically, than I listened at first. Even the poorer ones are opportunities for you to pull his image into a sharper focus in your own heart and mind.

After all, isn't Jesus' life so worth listening to? Millions, even billions, of us have given ear to it, charged by his Spirit who allows us to listen to his Word in a way we listen to nothing else in this world. Could it be that it also makes us, invites us, to resonate in a way in which we resonate to nothing else in this world? The Spirit strikes or hammers or plucks an interior place, and we resonate, we harmonize, something sings the way the morning stars first sang (Job 38:7).

There are still a million questions that have yet to be asked of Jesus' life. Many, most, are unanswerable, but that does not mean they are not worth asking. Even the unanswerable ones leave us with a sense of wonder, and that wonder just might enable us to keep asking better questions still. There are perhaps as many songs left to be written about his luminous life as have been written. If this book provides the encouragement for just one new song to even find the beginning it will have served its purpose.

PART I

MATTHEW
The Penultimate Question

HE SITS IN THE BACK CORNER of a black basalt synagogue somewhere in ancient Galilee. Since no one is looking, he steals a few moments in the "seat of Moses," but finds it so uncomfortable he moves to one of the back benches to work on his manuscript. His friends keep coming to him with the same sad story. Upon having realized that Jesus of Nazareth was the true Messiah, their Jewish friends and family have cast them out, banned them from Jewish life, and now, outside of the Jewish community, they simply don't know who they are anymore.

So here he sits, Levi, the cherished nickname Jesus himself had given Matthew. He struggles and strains and prays to remember everything Jesus said that might help his confused and wounded parishioners.

"*You are the light of the world*," he gasps. "Yes, that will help them understand who they are."

And after a few moments, "Oh yes and, '*you are the salt of the earth . . .*' That will encourage them as well."

And so Matthew Levi weaves together his inspired narrative of the life of his friend Jesus with the needs of his fellow Galilean Jews fresh in his mind. Though he himself is present in the story from chapter 9, he never opens his mouth. (Indeed, in none of the Gospels does he speak.) We know he walked away from his lucrative tax-gathering business in order to throw an extravagant party for Jesus. In light of his silence, perhaps that's all we need to know about Matthew.

Later, Papias will tell us Matthew collected the sayings (*logia*) of Jesus. That makes sense, a tax collector collecting sayings. When we open his Gospel, we see five large blocks of the sayings of Jesus. Just flip through a red-letter Bible and the structure becomes obvious: five blocks, like the five books of Moses. His confused and excluded followers would have appreciated that structure. It was so much a part of the world they were now excluded from.

On that luminous day at the banquet in his spacious Capernaum home, Levi remembered sitting in a corner amid the festivities and asking himself, "Who am I *now*?" His little band of ostracized Jewish followers of Jesus are now asking themselves the selfsame question. They simply don't know who they are anymore without their Jewish homes and families and synagogues.

"Who am I?" In time Matthew realized, though it was a good question, it still was not the best. In fact, he would say it was the next to the best one; it was the *penultimate* question. The first, ultimate question, in fact the only question that really matters in the end, is, *Who is Jesus?*

The sound echoes in the empty stone room as Matthew claps his hands and exclaims, "That's what they need!" And so, in his perfect account of the life of Christ, whenever the question

"Who am I?" is implied between the lines of the text, Matthew provides the answer to the better question we should have asked in the first place. He tells us who Jesus is.

2

THIS IS WHO YOU ARE

Matthew 5:10; 19:14

Misunderstood and undefined, a stranger to myself
Incarnate contradiction, I am poverty and wealth
I can believe and disbelieve
I can bless and I can damn
I'm dying in the darkness
Of not knowing who I am
Then rising like the morning sun, the light begins to speak
In a voice that's vastly strong yet still so infinitely weak
It's roaring like a lion
It whispers like a lamb
It's thundering that who you are
Is wrapped in who I am
   You possess the kingdom
   You are the sorrowful, the meek
   The gentle starving ones
   Who are the strongest when you're weak
   You're always making peace each time
   You suffer for what's right
   You freely offer mercy
   From a heart I filled with light
To everyone who's lost he gives a new identity
That's grounded in the kingdom and a new reality

It's found in lovingkindness
And a mercy that is free
You can become the child
That you were always meant to me
   The flavor of my world comes through
   The seasoning of your life
   Remember when the darkness looms
   You were meant to be the light
   A light that can't be hidden
   All will see it from afar
   This is who you are

THIS IS WHO YOU ARE

Imagine you are a young Jew who has heard the message of the gospel, and it has exploded in your heart and life. You continue to attend synagogue. Scattered within the congregation are others like yourself who have come to believe in Jesus of Nazareth as the Messiah. There are even synagogues built by the Nazarenes—*Christian* synagogues! As perplexing as this sounds, it aligns with what we see in the New Testament, not a monolithic Judaism but what Jewish scholar Isaiah Gafni calls "Judaisms." A synagogue contingent led by Pharisees, a temple group led by Sadducees, and Essenes who don't want to have anything to do with any of them, a large group of the followers of John the Baptist, and finally a small but dedicated group of the followers of the Way, a sect also referred to as the Nazarenes.

In AD 70, with the destruction of Jerusalem and the temple by Titus, all that changed. The temple was gone and so were the priests and the Sadducees. The Essenes were slaughtered. What survived was the synagogue, with scattered communities all over the country led by the Pharisees. The task now was to unite Judaism. Part of the unifying process necessitated expelling the followers of Jesus from the community. But how best to accomplish this when they are so firmly entrenched in the synagogue? In fact, the deepest belief of many of the early Christians is that in order to become a follower of Jesus one must first be a Jew; that is, Gentiles are generally disqualified unless they become full converts. That will change later with Peter and Paul.

The Romans realized that the Pharisees posed no threat and permitted them to retreat to the city of Javneh and piece together what was left of their decimated faith. There they hit upon the solution of how to exclude the Nazarenes. As they formulated the basic elements of the synagogue service, they developed what has come to be known as the Eighteen Benedictions or the Amidoth. They are, for the most part, the most beautiful collection of blessings you will ever hear. Just listen to the first benediction:

> O L-rd open my lips, and my mouth shall declare your praise. Blessed art thou, O L-rd our G-d and G-d of our fathers, G-d of Abraham, G-d of Isaac, and G-d of Jacob, the great and mighty, the revered G-d, the most high G-d, who bestows lovingkindness, and the Master of all things; who remembers the pious deeds of the patriarchs, and in love will bring a Redeemer to their children's children for your Name's sake.

Or the fifth:

> Cause us to return, our Father, unto Your Torah; draw us near, our King, unto Your service, and bring us back in perfect repentance unto Your presence, Blessed art Thou, O L-rd, who delights in repentance.

But now listen to the twelfth, which was added at Javneh:

And for the slanderers let there be no hope, and let all wick-
edness perish as in a moment; let all Your enemies be speedily
cut off, and the dominion of arrogance uproot and crush,
cast down and humble speedily in our days. Blessed art Thou,
O L-rd, who breaks the enemies and humbles the arrogant.

This twelfth benediction was a litmus test for the followers of
Jesus who tried to remain. It was thought that no one would know-
ingly curse themselves and so as the congregation pronounced the
Eighteen Benedictions (now there were nineteen), suspected followers were closely watched when they came to the twelfth benediction. This is the life situation of Matthew's first readers. They
are under suspicion. They are being expelled from Jewish life, and
consequently they don't know who they are anymore.

In a world that had branded them heretics, *minim*, Matthew recognized the need to tell his troubled congregation just who Jesus
had said they were. Only Matthew recalls Jesus telling his followers
that they were the "light of the world," "the salt of the earth." The
kingdom (his major theme) was theirs, and most importantly, Jesus
was their King!

♫ LYRIC NOTE ♫

This is who you are

The title is the key lyric to this song, which is often the case. It pulls
together all the different descriptions in the previous lyrics that describe who we are meant to become in Christ. The placement of
this line at the very end of the song, as well as at the end of a second,
different chorus, is meant to give it added power and emphasis.

3

GALILEE

THE BEAUTY OF GALILEE is beyond words. So it was necessary to make this an instrumental. In contrast to the desert surrounding Jerusalem to the south in Judea, Galilee is green and fertile. I like to think of it as Jesus' world.

Galilee is the major flyway between Africa and Europe. Flocks of every imaginable species of bird are funneled over the verdant countryside. Storks and cranes pass through the country twice a year on their way to winter in Africa or to escape the heat and nest in Europe. There are also the indigenous birds that stay for the most part—beautiful green long-tailed parakeets, iridescent kingfishers and larks, Egyptian vultures and cormorants. My favorite is the wagtail, which is and does exactly what its name implies. It makes me wonder if Jesus had a favorite. If he laughed quietly to himself as the wagtails made their comical way across an open field, wagging their tails as they went.

Then there are the orchards, the vineyards, the figs, and the olives, for Galilee is an amazingly fertile land. The fields are a marvelous mixture of impossible rockiness and fertility. The contours of those green hillsides—they were his world, a beauty his eyes took in every morning. And the sunsets . . . Galilee is a place of almost daily magnificent sunsets.

Three and sometimes four times a year, Jesus would leave this beautiful green place and wander down through the desolate wilderness that surrounded Jerusalem, a city that was in and of itself a sort of wilderness in Jesus' day. How much did he miss the cool lake breezes as he and the Twelve bedded down in the Judean desert? Or did his calling and purpose completely override any homesickness for the beautiful lush land they had left in the north?

And finally, there is the lake, Kinnereth or Galilee or Tiberius. It is almost as if it is so beautiful no one could decide on what to call it. The shoals of fish, the glistening reflections of sunrises and sunsets, even the comfortable, comprehensible size of it. Some see the outline of the shoreline in the shape of the human heart, and that makes sense. The lake is the beating heart of Galilee and the heart of Jesus' world.

4

A SIMPLE HOUSE

Matthew 2:1-12

It seemed an endless journey
Looking for the Holy Child
So many times, we thought the signs had lied
Till in Nazareth we found the boy
Just as He had started walking
A Child so fair we hardly could believe
    The prophets told us He'd be coming
    But we never did believe
    Till we saw the star of Jacob in the east
    Casting light upon our way
    Shining brighter than the moon
    Above a simple house in Galilee
Like any other boy
He was always on the move
And into everything that He could find
But the look upon His face
As we offered Him our gifts
Made us know for certain
Jesus was a King
All along the lonely miles
We were wondering all the while
Is this little boy, a king
Our final answer?

A SIMPLE HOUSE

When it comes to the nativity of Jesus, very little is as it seems. In the first place we have lumped together Matthew's and Luke's accounts, making them one story when in fact they might have been separated by a year or more. In Luke the baby Jesus is impoverished, sleeping in a stone trough, being worshiped by humble shepherds. Most importantly, he is a newborn. When Joseph and Mary have completed all of the Jewish rituals associated with the birth of Jesus, Luke 2:39 tells us they returned to Nazareth. That is, they went home.

In Matthew he is a young King, being worshiped by wise men from Persia, the kingmakers of their country. And they are giving him kingly gifts: gold and costly incense. Significantly, he is not a newborn but a "young child." I believe the house they are living in, which Matthew refers to, is in Nazareth. But following the golden rule of interpreting the Bible, "Never be dogmatic about what the Bible is not dogmatic about!" I would never argue this point. It just makes the most sense to me given the language of both Gospels.

No matter where it was, nor even exactly how old Jesus was, the point is his kingship is recognized by those whose role it was to recognize kings. They have come to acknowledge him as such and honor him with the kinds of gifts you give to kings, gifts which will probably provide resources for the holy family's escape and sojourn in Egypt.

The wise men have seen an unusual star. It seems to have appeared the moment Jesus was born and guided them on the long journey from Persia. This is another part of the story we tend to confuse. Planetariums all over the country run their "Star of Bethlehem" programs, explaining that what probably led the wise men on their journey was a complex conjunction of two or more planets in the constellation Pegasus, known in Judaism as the "House of the Hebrews." But it should be blatantly obvious that a stellar object, that is, one in the celestial sphere, could not be followed in such a way.

Like the sun and the moon, stars rise in the east and set in the west, impossible to follow. Also, if you go outside at night and simply look up at the stars you will realize that it would be impossible for something so far away to indicate a single, individual house, the way the Star of Bethlehem did. Once more, I would never dogmatically argue the point, but it seems to me that what led the wise men was in fact an angel. Angels are sometimes referred to as stars in Scripture (Judg 5:20; Job 38:7; Is 14:12; Rev 1:20; 8:10; 12:4).

We could analyze and debate the details endlessly, but what we need to extract from the nativity of Matthew is the essence of what's being said to us, what the Spirit is saying to us. Clearly what interests Matthew most is the fact that Jesus is a king, and so the kingdom becomes his major theme. He emphasizes the fact of the kingdom to his early readers because they are being excluded from Jewish life and feel as if they have no place to go.

Matthew's point, made again and again throughout his Gospel, is that though they may have been excluded from the Jewish community, they indeed have a kingdom. And the central point of Matthew's nativity is that Jesus is the King of that kingdom.

♫ LYRIC NOTE ♫

Made us know for certain, Jesus was a king.

This might not be my favorite line of the song, the most poetic or compelling, but it contains the idea that pulls the whole lyric, as well as the story of the wise men, together. They journeyed for months, some say years, following the star and looking for the new king. What was their level of anticipation? How long could they hold on to the hope that they would finally find the king? And when they finally did find him, in such unlikely circumstances, what was the attitude of their hearts?

5

AND DREAMED

That night when in Judean skies
The wondrous star did shine so bright
A blind man moved while in his sleep
And dreamed that he had sight

That night when Magi traveled far
While o'er the house the star drew near
A deaf man stirred in slumber's spell
And dreamed that he could hear

That night when safe in Joseph's arms
The little King was held secure
A captive child smiled in her sleep
And dreamed that she was pure

That night when o'er the newborn Babe
The tender Mary rose to lean
A leper slept a happy sleep
And dreamed that he was clean

And all the while the dreamers dreamed
The Child who would redeem them
Lay weeping for the world
He would waken

That night when in the manger lay
The Son of God who came to save
A man moved in the sleep of death
And dreamed that there was no grave

AND DREAMED

Poems and lyrics are the best vehicles for hope, both to instill and to celebrate it. A few weeks before her death I asked my mother, a great lover of poetry, if she had a favorite. Lying there in her sickbed, she recited in total and from memory the original version of this poem. (I later reshaped it into a lyric form.) The name of the original poet has been lost.

It is brilliant in its structure and simplicity, centering on the hopes and dreams of five people: a blind man, a deaf man, a "captive" child (in the original poem it was a prostitute), a leper, and finally a corpse. The recurring theme that holds the lyric together is their dream of finding healing for their disease and disability. The blind man dreams of sight. The deaf man of hearing. The child of a restored purity. The leper of cleansing. Appearing as he does at the end of the song, the lyric focuses on the dead man, who dreams of a time when there will be no need of graves.

Part of the elegance of the poem is that in the Gospels Jesus actually encounters each of them and heals or raises or restores their purity. So, we know how their stories will end if we've read the Gospels.

The fifth section of the lyric, which functions as a chorus or perhaps a bridge, cuts to the manger where the infant Jesus lies crying as the others simultaneously dream their dreams. Only he is awake. He is not dreaming like the others. He is weeping for them and for the whole disabled and diseased and captive world. Buried deep within the words is the notion that the wailing infant will someday waken all us dreamers to a real, wide-awake world that is clean and healed and whole. That hope lies deep in the lyric of his life.

♫ *LYRIC NOTE* ♫

This poem relies on an elegant structure. The five characters are held together by their activity of dreaming. Yet their dreams are all different, according to their individual needs. The contrast of the awake and weeping Jesus, who will eventually perfectly meet all their needs, is what gives the lyric its power.

6

HIS HUMANITY

Born in flesh, like you and me
In His humanity
To be believed, for all to see
Was His identity
In flesh and blood, in tender skin
His birth begins the story
From an empty grave He rose to save
And this became the beginning of good news.
His familiar voice, its changing tones
His laugh, His groan, His smile
All the sleepless nights, His lonely grief
Their disbelief, His sighs
His homelessness, His weariness
Asleep on a stormy sea
Soaked by the rain, while in His veins
His blood contained the hope
For all the world
He was hungry, He was happy
He was tired, He was thirsty
He could sorrow, He could savor
He could marvel at the flowers
He could thrill hearing birds sing
He could weep at the first sign of spring
His hour had come, and far too soon

With the waxing of the moon
Caught up in a tide of hate and lies
A torrent toward the tomb
Midst the pain and fear
His joyful tears
Were blended with His bleeding
In the endless ache His eyes await
And dilate with the darkness
He is bleeding, He is pleading
He is crying, He is dying
As He fights to go on breathing
His mind sees each soul
He will redeem
Music by Scott Brasher

HIS HUMANITY

Was Jesus' heart rate more or less than the normal 60-80 bpm? Did it quicken when he was excited and slow when he took a deep breath to relax? What about his cholesterol level? Was it a healthy 100 or higher? Given the nature of a first-century diet, my guess is high cholesterol didn't pose too much of a threat. And what about his fingerprints? Were they simple loops, or the rarer circular pattern? What color were his eyes?

These may seem like fruitless, frivolous questions, and of course we cannot know the answers to them yet, but for me, unanswerable questions still matter. Socrates said, "Sometimes there is more knowing in the questions than in the answers." All these unanswerable questions point to his humanity, his complete, perfect experience of all that it means to be human. His eyes dilated with the darkness. His skin bruised when he struck his knee against the corner of a chair.

He almost certainly inherited mannerisms from Mary and adopted those of Joseph: his laugh, his smile, the way he would lean his head to one side when he was thinking deeply about something.

We know from the Gospels that he was hungry (Mt 4:2; 21:18), that he was tired (Jn 4:6), that he was a deep sleeper (Lk 8:23). He marveled; I cannot imagine Jesus not being drawn to the breathtaking beauty of Galilee, to the myriad birds and flowers, to the beauty of the lake.

Exercising our imaginations in wondering about the extent of the humanity of Jesus may draw us to him in a new and more particular way, but it misses the central point. Whatever the blood type that flowed through his veins, it was the sacrifice of that blood that redeemed and paid for the sins of the world.

> While in His veins
> His blood contained
> the hope for all the world.

He lived a fully—yet perfect—human life. As the author of Hebrews reminds us, he was tempted in every way just as we are, yet without sin. It qualifies him not simply to be our great high priest but moreover to be the perfect sacrifice. That was the point of his humanity.

♫ *LYRIC NOTE* ♫

His mind sees each soul He will redeem

While I love the idea of the blood flowing in his veins containing the hope for the world, for me the song turns on the moment when, on the cross, Jesus perceives each person his suffering will redeem. The most striking line is not always necessarily the key.

7

The GIFT to BELIEVE

Matthew 6:25-34

Jesus said, Do not worry
About what to eat and wear
If you will seek the Kingdom
My love will calm your fear
Look at the birds
I made them and keep them
And like them I want you to be
Faith is the gift to believe
Each day is full of trouble
I want you to bring them to me
I am your great Provider
I know your every need
Look at the lilies
They never labor
Yet what a splendor to see
Faith is the gift to believe
Worry can never provide
Or add a day to your life
Seek first the Kingdom
And His righteousness
And you will have all you need

> *Faith is the gift to believe*
> *So take no thought for tomorrow*
> *Each day has cares enough of its own*
> *So live for the Kingdom*
> *Your heart will be free*
> *There your treasure will be*
> *Faith is the gift to believe*
> Cowritten with Scott Roley

THE GIFT TO BELIEVE

In Matthew 5:1-2 Jesus sits down (a sign that he is going to teach) and teaches "them." The "them" is probably the disciples who are gathered around him. In my imagination the enormous crowd of thousands are there for the most part, not to listen to him teach but rather to be healed or fed. Matthew lets us know that even though it is early in his ministry, Jesus already has been teaching, preaching, and healing "all over Galilee" (Mt 4:23). The crowds are coming from as far away as Jerusalem.

He begins the lengthy teaching session with what we call the Beatitudes, but more precisely they are his innovative eight blessings or benedictions. Matthew gives them in distinction to the recent innovation in Judaism called the Eighteen Benedictions.

About halfway through the Sermon on the Mount, in Matthew 6:25, Jesus provides a list of the things they need to stop worrying about: their life, what they will eat or drink or wear. Appealing to their Jewish identities he says these are the things that the Gentiles worry about. There is only one thing that they need to "worry about" (or seek) and that is the kingdom, Matthew's major theme.

In Jesus' remarkable kingdom there is no place for worry. To worry about food or clothing implies a lack of confidence in the King. Remember that Jesus preaches the sermon in Galilee, an area filled with all kinds of birds. There is every likelihood that the air around him is filled with the songs of birds as Jesus directs the disciples' attention to them. The birds don't worry about anything because apparently they have learned to trust their Creator. Even the insensible lilies, clothed in such gorgeous colors, don't worry about what they wear. After all, worry accomplishes absolutely nothing except to distract the disciples from the one thing they should be seeking and that is Jesus' kingdom.

Throughout the Gospels Jesus says, "Do not worry" eleven times. He encourages the disciples not to be afraid nine times. Remembering that the Gospels represent an excruciatingly small slice of the life of Jesus (someone has estimated .09 percent), in reality he must have been constantly encouraging them to take their eyes off their situations and look to him and the coming of his great kingdom.

♫ LYRIC NOTE ♫

Worry can never provide

While the title is the foundation to the lyric, this line sums up the application in a succinct way. It is placed at the opening of the bridge at a time when the music lifts, which reinforces its message.

8

WHEN DID WE SEE YOU?

Matthew 25:31-46

When He comes in glory, with His holy ones
To separate the nations and call us one by one
Come, you child of God the kingdom is at hand
The inheritance I've held for you is now the Promised Land
For I was hungry, lost and tired, a stranger, all alone
In a cold dark prison cell, no place to call my own
When did we see you among the least of these?
For when you gave a stranger love
You gave it all to me
He divides the people like darkness from light
The goats and sheep are kept apart
As His left is from His right
Away from me you'll go, no kingdom, only fire
Without my Presence and my love
To quench your deep desire
When did we see you among the least of these
For when you did not give your love
You did not give to me (repeat)
Cowritten with Scott Roley

WHEN DID WE SEE YOU?

This teaching comes at the other end of the ministry of Jesus, only a few days before the final Passover. For the most part we have only a rough idea of the settings of his Galilean teachings. They take place on a remote hillside or somewhere beside the lake. At most we know the name of the vicinity or perhaps the town Jesus is in.

But in Jerusalem we can usually pinpoint his location, be it Solomon's colonnade or the steps on the southern side of the temple mount. The Matthew 25:31-46 teaching is no exception. In Matthew 24:3 we read that Jesus is sitting on the Mount of Olives, and what is most significant about this location is the view. To the west on the temple mount stands what would've been one of the seven wonders of the world if it had been around at the time when Herodotus made his famous list. What is rarely spoken of in regards to Herod's temple is that it was a popular tourist attraction, even in the first century AD. People would come from as far away as Rome to see the magnificent structure regardless of whether they were practicing Jews or not.

From the Mount of Olives they would have seen the smoke rising from the sacrificial altar in front of the temple, perhaps even smelling the sacrifice itself if the wind was blowing in the right direction. They would have heard sporadic bursts of music as seven times a day the Levitical band would play. And since Passover was only a few days away, the thirty-five-acre plaza around the temple would have been packed with pilgrims from all over the world. That view, those sounds and smells, are the backdrop for these words of Jesus, a lesson that concerns a great separation that will come some day, saints and sinners as sheep and goats.

The teaching is found in Matthew's final block of the five collections of the sayings of Jesus. This story, the division between the sheep and the goats, is presented as Jesus' last lesson in Matthew's Gospel. Given the life situation of his first readers, it takes on a whole new significance.

When we remember Matthew's Gospel is written to Jewish believers in Jesus who are being excluded from the community because of their newfound faith, we will hear a new tone of hope in this unique story that perhaps we have never heard before. If you, and perhaps even your family, had been kicked out of the synagogue because of your belief in the Messiah Jesus, how would you have received this message of the separation of the sheep and goats?

What I find most intriguing about this parable is the fact that both groups, the sheep as well as the goats, are confused. One group has neglected to do what they should've done and remains unaware while the other group did precisely what they should've done and yet also remains clueless. Both groups had been confronted with the poor in various states of distress. They had both encountered people who were hungry and thirsty, who were strangers, who were sick, homeless, in prison, and even naked. The group on the right side, the sheep, intuitively acted out of kindness and fed and watered and healed and clothed and provided homes for the needy. Jesus, represented by the king in the story, responds to their confused question, "When did we see you?" with the surprising answer that whenever they were caring for the poor, it was really Jesus the King they were ministering to.

To those on the left, the goats, Jesus pronounces a parallel yet negative version of what he'd said to the sheep. This group on the left side is also confused, yet for the precisely opposite reason. They had failed to care for the poor in every imaginable dimension. They had not fed or clothed or housed or visited anyone. Apparently, they had been presented with the same group of naked, homeless poor as the group standing on the right side, yet they did nothing. Once again Jesus radically identifies with the poor when he says, "*I* was hungry . . . *I* was thirsty." Then comes the surprising twist. In neglecting the poor it was in fact Jesus the King they were neglecting.

The final moment of separation occurs in verse 46. The group on the left, the goats, will be driven to eternal punishment while the group on the right, the sheep, will be ushered into eternal life. If you and I were part of Matthew's original audience, if we were being excluded from the synagogue and being kicked out of Jewish life, we might be tempted to become so concerned about our own lives that we might forget the poor and the needy, with whom Jesus stands in radical solidarity.

Perhaps Matthew had this in mind when he remembered these words of Jesus. They are unique to Matthew's Gospel. Only he seems to have remembered this parable of Jesus as he was collecting the *logia* or sayings of Jesus that Papias tells us he recorded in the middle of the second century AD.

♫ **LYRIC NOTE** ♫

For when you did not give your love
You did not give to me

This line is the key because it sums up the message. The punchline of the parable of the sheep and goats is the moment Jesus separates the two groups, on his left and right, on the basis of how they treated the poor, the hungry, and the prisoner. The powerful twist of his story is when he radically identifies himself with those three suffering groups. The goal of the lyric is to capture the power of that pivotal statement.

9

GO FIND OUT WHAT
THIS MEANS

Matthew 9:13; 12:8

Matthew waiting, sittin' by the sea
Jesus called, and said, "Come and follow me."
The sinners celebrated that he had been set free
The scribes and the teachers scorned their company
   So go find out, go find out what this means
   Jesus told the self-righteous Pharisees
   "I desire mercy, not sacrifice to me"
   So go find out, go find out what this means
The starved disciples eat their grain from their hands
All the scribes can see is a broken command
And I want your lovingkindness, not your disbelieving demands
For your mercy completes all the commands
   So go find out, go find out what this means
   Jesus told the self-righteous Pharisees
   "I desire mercy, not sacrifice to me"
   So go find out, go find out what this means
kee hesed hapatz tee (For mercy I desire)
va low zavach (and not sacrifice) [Hosea 6:6]
Go find out, go find out what this means
Jesus told the self-righteous Pharisees

> "*I desire mercy, not sacrifice to me*"
> *So go find out, go find out what this means*

GO FIND OUT WHAT THIS MEANS

Jesus' relationship with the Pharisees, the powerful "back to the Bible" group of his day, is far more complex than most people realize. Certainly, he frequently comes into conflict with them, and that is our dominant impression. But in some ways Jesus was like the Pharisees. He believed and taught the resurrection, which was a core tenet of the Pharisees' teaching. (The Sadducees and the priests denied the possibility of resurrection.) Jesus quoted the Prophets and occasionally even the Wisdom Writings, which was a very pharisaic thing to do. He was occasionally called "rabbi," which was a new innovation of the pharisaic movement. And finally, until his movement outgrew the synagogue, Jesus based his ministry there, the power base of the Pharisees.

In two separate scenes in Matthew, Jesus tries to correct the Pharisees. I don't believe his tone was necessarily condemning. We are too quick to assume that would have always been his posture because it probably would have been ours. But in both cases Jesus' response can be read as calm, even encouraging.

In the first scene, in the midst of a collection of miracle stories, Matthew tells the story of the miracle of his own coming to Jesus. Luke tells us he put on a "grand banquet." In the celebration there appears to have been a small clutch of the most severe Pharisees, the followers of Shammai, who follow Jesus virtually everywhere he goes. They seem to be scrutinizing his every move, waiting for him to violate their oral law (which he does every chance he gets). This group, probably huddled at the door because they would have never entered unclean Matthew's house, look inside and see Jesus sharing the intimacy of meal fellowship with Matthew and his dubious friends, reclining at the table. Matthew gives the detail that the Pharisees' question, "Why does your teacher eat with sinners?" is directed toward Jesus' disciples. Maybe a few of them are standing outside as well, not yet willing to join their rabbi!

Understand, within the context of Jewish culture it is a perfectly legitimate concern. Ritual purity was an important element of the culture of Judaism. Jesus' point really concerns his understanding of Torah, of what, at its heart, the Law is really saying. In forty years one of the greatest first-century rabbis, Yohanan ben Zakkai, will make a similar point, quoting the exact passage from Hosea.

"Go and learn what this means," Jesus says. "*I desire kindness and not sacrifice*" (Mt 9:13, quoting Hos 6:6).

In his mind Jesus believes that his kindness and openness to Matthew and his questionable friends, an openness that just might lead them to the kingdom, are more desirable in God's eyes than offering a sacrifice. Jesus suggests that the studious Pharisees go back to their Bibles and look into it. Perhaps, then, Jesus' words were not spoken in anger. They may very well have been friendly encouragement.

In the second incident Jesus and his disciples are walking through one of many green fields in the fertile Galilee. So hungry are they that the raw heads of grain look appealing, and they begin to pluck and eat the raw grain. To the Pharisees this looks like work, harvesting, and Matthew tells us it is the Sabbath (Mt 12:1).

Jesus, who lived a perfect, sinless life, never breaking the law, has not violated Torah. Provision is made for the poor to glean from the corners of the field, and since they aren't using metal tools, it is not regarded in the law of Moses as harvesting. And besides, says Jesus, "haven't you read . . . ?" Oh boy, *have they read*, they have strained at every jot and tittle of the law, which means they know intimately the story from 1 Samuel 21 that Jesus refers to. They know that the priests allowed David and his men to eat the bread of the Presence, which is reserved only for the priests. But David and his men had consecrated themselves, and like Jesus and the Twelve, they too were on a mission.

What's more, says Jesus, the priests in the temple work on the Sabbath, do they not? Something greater than the temple is here, Jesus says, no doubt referring to himself and the kingdom of God he is ushering in along with himself.

He makes the same point he made in chapter 9. If only they understood the passage in Hosea, their hypocrisy would be cured and they could see clearly what God was doing. He desires kindness before sacrifice.

Hesed is the word for kindness or mercy Hosea uses. It is one of the words God uses to define himself in Exodus 34:6. It is the closest Jesus comes to proposing the cure for the hypocrisy of the Pharisees. The remedy is simple kindness. In all the Gospels we only hear this precious word from Jesus' lips twice, and they are here in these two run-ins with the Pharisees.

♫ LYRIC NOTE ♫

And I want your lovingkindness, not your disbelieving demands
For your mercy completes all the commands

This line comes in the middle of the song and sums up the passage
the song is based on, Hosea 6:6. "I desire *hesed* and not sacrifice."
Since this is the passage Jesus quotes to the Pharisees, this para-
phrase of that line makes it the key.

10

THE KINGDOM

Matthew 4:23; 6:33; 7:21; 13:11, 31, 44-45; 19:14

So near and yet still so far, far away
So close, and yet still to come
Concealed, the seed is mysteriously growing
In hearts that will listen and hear
A treasure that's hidden, a pearl of great price
A fortune for fools who believe
   A kingdom of beauty, a kingdom of love
   A kingdom of justice and peace
   A kingdom that holds all the wilds of creation
   A kingdom where children will lead
For now, this kingdom's a land of the lowly
A place for the tired, plundered poor
Now our gentle King comes in peace on a donkey
But then on a charger for war
A battle in heaven, a war on the earth
To shatter the long, darkened siege
   Not by our own strength
   And not by power of might
   But by His Spirit it comes
   Blinded eyes will see
   And deafened ears will hear

The praise from the lips of the dumb
Music by Scott Brasher

THE KINGDOM

John's Gospel mentions the kingdom only three times. Matthew, however, refers to it fifty-four times! His disenfranchised Jewish community feels as if they have no place to call home, no place to go. Matthew rallies all of Jesus' sayings concerning the kingdom to let his frail followers in Galilee know that they belong to a kingdom and that Jesus is their King.

The concept of kingdom is complex and deep. We want it to mean one thing, one literal translatable word, but there's far more to it than that. In the Gospels it *has* come and *is* coming, the now and the not yet. It is close and yet far away. It is a seed, a pearl. At one point, Jesus says it is full of secrets (Mt 13:11). He alludes to the fact that, in one sense, it is him! What could be more significant than Jesus' words in Matthew 6:33 that we must seek the kingdom first, above all else. It is that important.

To the more verbal Hebrew mind the kingdom is not so much a place (that is, a noun) as it normally appears to us. *Kingdom* is almost a verb in Hebrew and can sometimes be translated "reign." When, in Luke's Gospel, Gabriel tells Mary that her son's kingdom will last forever, he is essentially saying that Jesus' reign will last forever. Jesus' kingdom is also his reign.

This helps us understand what the good news of the kingdom is all about. After all, it is the principal message Jesus comes preaching in Matthew 4:23 and 9:35, and it is also the message he sends the Twelve and the Seventy out to preach. Quite simply the good news of the kingdom is that Jesus' reign has begun and will never end!

One of the images Jesus uses to describe this complex notion of the kingdom is that of a treasure hidden in a field (Mt 13:44). The man who discovers the hidden treasure sells everything he has to obtain it—with joy, Jesus adds. The merchant in the very next story does the same thing to purchase the pearl, which is the kingdom. And then, without a blink, Jesus says the kingdom is like a net that catches every imaginable sort of fish, which must be sorted out in a judgment motif. The kingdom is like a tiny mustard seed that promises so little by its smallness but produces an extraordinarily large plant.

The kingdom is hidden and revealed, small and enormous, close and far away. Jesus says when you're close to him, you are close to the kingdom. It has come, and it is coming. It is here and will be here. Very soon! To the demoralized Galilean Jews in Matthew's community, what mattered most was the good news of this mysterious kingdom. The good news? They had a king: Jesus was his name, and his reign had begun if not in Galilee certainly within their hearts.

♫ *LYRIC NOTE* ♫

Blinded eyes will see
And deafened ears will hear
The praise from the lips of the dumb

This line comes at the end of the final bridge as the music builds and flows into the last chorus. It is key because it describes the effect of the coming of the kingdom, an effect we have seen throughout the Gospels in the healing ministry of Jesus. The twist that also makes this line a key is its description of the interaction of those who are healed by the coming of the kingdom. The blind and deaf will not simply see and hear, but they will now be able to perceive the praise that comes from the lips of those who were previously unable to speak!

PART II

MARK
The Beginning of the Gospel

I IMAGINE HIM YOUNG, impressionable, sitting at the feet of Peter, who called him his "son" (1 Pet 5:13). Eusebius tells us some members of the church had been urging him to write down Peter's testimony before it was too late and the Roman persecution caught up to him (Eusebius, "The Apostles," *Church History* 2.14). Which it eventually did. The persecution had begun, and it was becoming obvious that Peter might not have long to live, which ended up being the case. So, in a very real sense, Mark's Gospel is Peter's story.

It could be said that the church started in his mother's home in Jerusalem. Not just the Jerusalem church, but *the* church. They pray there when Peter is in prison. I like to think that Jesus' Last Supper was held there as well and that the young man carrying water back to the house was Mark himself (Mk 14:13). Without a doubt, when Peter is busted out of prison by the angel in Acts 12:12, it is Mark's house he flees to.

Paul tells us that the remarkable early church leader Barnabas is Mark's cousin (Col 4:10), and that Paul and Barnabas took Mark along with them on their first missionary journeys until there was a disagreement between the two regarding Mark himself. When their journey turned inland to Perga, the young Mark decided he had had enough and went home. His uncle Barnabas understood the young man's dilemma, forgave him, and eventually took him along on later missionary journeys. Paul, however, never understood and parted ways with Barnabas over the disagreement. He did eventually forgive Mark, however. In 2 Timothy 4:11, he asks Mark to rejoin him in Rome.

The cousin of Barnabas, he traveled with Paul as well as Peter, and the church began in his home: what better credentials could the writer of the first Gospel possess? The chronicles of Jesus' life began with his pen, in fact *Gospel* was a new literary form Mark invented. Paul speaks of the gospel but Mark writes *a* Gospel, the very first one, around AD 64, just after the great fire in Rome. It is the beginning of the telling of the story of Jesus, the very beginning. It is the beginning of a new literary form, the story of Jesus' life based on confession. It is the beginning, for those of us who are not eyewitnesses, to have a chance to really know Jesus of Nazareth. And Mark's Gospel is where it all began. It's appropriate that he should have written those words because the gospel, in one sense, began with him: "The *beginning* of the gospel of Jesus Christ" (Mk 1:1).

11

The BEGINNING of the GOSPEL

Mark 1:1; 8:29; 15:39

> The beginning of the Gospel
> Of Jesus Christ, the Son of God
> The beginning of the Good News
> Of Christ, the Son of God
> It was the question
> Of all questions
> A demand to comprehend the price
> And the answer
> Of all answers
> You are the Christ
> Standing in the
> Cross's shadow
> Of the death-drenched deed
> That he had done
> The response to the wordless question
> Surely this is God's own Son

THE BEGINNING OF THE GOSPEL

The opening verse of the gospel of Mark is also the table of contents. The entire Gospel is structured around two confessions: the confession of Peter in Caesarea Philippi (Mk 8:29) that Jesus is the Christ, and the confession of the centurion who crucified Jesus (Mk 15:39) that he is the Son of God. Hence in Mark the first words we hear are "The beginning of the good news of Jesus Christ, the Son of God." Mark's is not simply the first of the four Gospels to be written. It is the first Gospel ever to be written, and these are the perfect words to open the first telling of the good news.

In the course of the flow of Jesus' ministry, Peter's confession in Caesarea Philippi represents a major turning point. Jesus takes his disciples far to the north into pagan territory. Not far from where they are standing is the temple of the god Pan, which was built in front of an enormous cave that was thought to be the entrance to Hades. Next to that was the temple of the dancing goats. Here priests would observe the movements of ritual goats in order to predict the future.

Later there would be a temple to Augustus constructed on the other side of the temple of Pan. In none of the Gospels is the reason for Jesus leading them there spelled out. Perhaps he knows that in the future they will be called upon to confess his name in the face of raw paganism, and Caesarea Philippi was the perfect place to start. Whatever the reason, after the confession of Peter, Jesus sets out on a direct route to Jerusalem and the cross. Luke says it this way: "He resolutely set his face for Jerusalem" (Lk 9:51).

The second and final confession to give shape to the structure of the Gospel of Mark is spoken quite literally in the shadow of the cross. Peter remembers details that are found in none of the other Gospels. For example, he knows that Simon of Cyrene, the man who helped Jesus carry his cross, is the father of two men who are known to the readers, Alexander and Rufus (Mk 15:21; see

Rom 16:13). Peter remembers the detail that two criminals are crucified on either side of Jesus. He remembers that the crowd was
yelling insults at him and shaking their heads. Finally, Peter remembers that at the moment the curtain of the temple was torn in
two, the centurion in charge of the detachment assigned the task
of crucifying Jesus made a remarkable confession when he witnessed the way Jesus died.

Typically, victims on the cross died with a hoarse whisper. We
are told in all three Synoptic Gospels that Jesus gave up his spirit
with a loud shout. The Roman soldier, who had seen hundreds,
perhaps even thousands, of men die on the cross, had never seen
anyone die like this. He is clearly moved. Then comes his confession. "Truly this man was the Son of God!"

Those two confessions are signposts in Mark's Gospel. They
provide his unique "confessional framework."

♫ *LYRIC NOTE* ♫

And the answer
Of all answers
You are the Christ

This lyric tries to portray the two-part confessional structure of
Mark. The two verses describe the confessions of Peter and
the centurion.

In the first confession Peter responds to Jesus' question, "Who do
people say I am?" The centurion, standing before the cross, might
also be seen as responding to an unspoken question, "Who is this
man who dies with a victorious shout?" The only possible answer
to either of those questions is the one Mark provides. Jesus is the
Christ, the Son of God (Mk 1:1).

12

A GREAT WIND, a GREAT CALM, a GREAT FEAR

Mark 4:35-41

A demonic shaking of the sea
Black leagues of open water wide
A legion of the darkest kind
Lurking on the other side
A hand outstretched against the gale
A voice that stills the tempest roar
As muzzled death is silenced there
By He who calms the storm
    A Great Wind, a Great Calm, a Great Fear
    An unspeakable Power is here
    Far beyond the darkness and the waves
    There is a very real reason to be afraid
In a question rising from the flood
Who is this man and what's this strength
The storms before His power still
And waters must obey
A shivering in the heart of man
Whose fearful faith is a facade
Now saved from fear and dark despair
To know the Son of God
Cowritten with Sarah Hart

A GREAT WIND, A GREAT CALM,
A GREAT FEAR

As Mark records the remembrances of Peter from time to time, he exercises some of his own literary muscle and Mark 4:35-41 is one of the best examples. The story of the demonic storm is a good example of the need to ignore chapter breaks in the Bible. They were only added in the sixteenth century and so should not be regarded as Holy Scripture. Admittedly they are helpful in finding our way around in the Bible, so that's a good thing, but occasionally they do more harm than good by dividing two stories that should be taken together. The division between chapters four and five in Mark unfortunately divides into two sections a story that can be properly understood only as a whole.

That this particular storm is demonic in nature and not meteorological is seen in the fact that Jesus says to the storm precisely what he says to demons when he exorcises them: "Be muzzled." Also, though many of the disciples had spent a lifetime on the Sea of Galilee and had no doubt seen the most severe storms, Mark implies that they've never seen a storm like this before. (Matthew refers to this particular storm as a *seismos* or "shaking" [Mt 8:24].) After the storm, Jesus is confronted with a demonized man from Gadara, a story that concludes with two thousand pigs floating dead on the surface of the lake.

The connections between the two stories become clear. The violent storm on the Sea of Galilee was a satanic attack on Jesus and the Twelve. What eventually happened to the herd of pigs in the end of the story was Satan's intention for Jesus and his disciples.

They were the ones who were supposed to be floating, drowned by the storm. But Jesus' disturbing, absolute authority over the wind and the waves overpowered the storm as it will always overpower the enemy of our souls.

Disturbing is the operative word, especially in Mark's rendition of this story. He makes a vital point concerning the story that none of the other Gospel writers choose to incorporate into their stories. And he uses something he rarely uses to make his point: poetry. This is where listening closely to the text makes all the difference.

My guess is this poetic device is an invention of Mark and not of Peter. I would like to believe that in telling the story, he listened to Peter's heart and expressed what was most important about the incident with his own poetic invention. He structures the story around three phrases: *megalae anamou, galanae megalae,* and *phobou megan.*

The parallelism is actually easier to perceive in translation than in the original Greek. In the course of telling the story Mark says there was a "great wind." Then after Jesus spoke there was a "great calm." And finally, among the disciples there was a "great fear." In fearful amazement the Twelve ask one another, "Who is this?" Jesus' authority over the wind and the sea is clearly disturbing to them. The amazing point of Mark's unique telling of the story is that it is not the storm that ultimately frightens the disciples, though indeed they had never seen anything to equal it; what frightened the disciples, according to Mark, is Jesus.

♫ *LYRIC NOTE* ♫

Far beyond the darkness and the waves
There is a very real reason to be afraid

The position of this key lyric is everything. It comes as the last line of the chorus. This song seeks to capture what is unique about Mark's telling of the demonic storm. This single line encapsulates that unique idea. It is not the storm the disciples fear at that moment . . . it is Jesus.

13

The SERVICE of
the SOD

Mark 4:1-32

The seed is scattered, it is sown
Though it has power of its own
The sower casts it all around
It falls upon the fallow ground
The sower sows in faithful toil
Some on rocky, shallow soil
Some eaten by the birds that swarm
Some is withered, choked by thorns
    The seed remains the same
      With the mystery of the power it contains
      But what produces fruit for God
      Is the service of the sod
Know the kingdom's come to you
If you have ears to hear the truth
If you have eyes that you might see
You are the soil meant for the seed
The mystery of the seed remains
It is so small and self-contained
The sower need not ascertain
And though he sleeps, produces grain

THE SERVICE OF THE SOD

The seed is the Word, the good news, the gospel, the message of the meaning of Jesus. It is what the Twelve were originally sent out to preach, to broadcast ("to cast abroad") and what we are empowered to preach with our lips and lives and hands and feet. In Jesus' parable the seed remains the same, but the soils are different: rocky, weedy, and finally fertile. Notice the detail in the parable that the seed always sprouts and grows. It always does what it is designed and empowered to do—it is good seed! Yet in the first two instances it does not produce a crop. That, it appears to me, is the fault of the soil. Or perhaps, if you read between the lines of Jesus' parable, it is the responsibility of the one who sowed the seed. Perhaps it is both. The seed has power of its own but the soil plays its part or not.

This is the only parable Jesus explains privately to the Twelve. It is vital they understand the dynamics of the seed and the soils because they are about to be sent out on their first mission to broadcast this powerful seed. They need to understand that some people's souls might best be described as rocky or full of weeds, and for some receiving the seed will probably not produce anything in their lives. Though not strictly implied in the parable (yet I really want it to be), fields can be rid of rocks and weeds so there will be other opportunities for the powerful seed to grow. We do learn from the parable that the seed sprouts in all three. So, there is always reason for hope.

John Bannister Tabb's powerful poem "Earth's Tribute" was a favorite of my Grandfather Brown.

First the grain, and then the blade—
The one destroyed, the other made;

Then stalk and blossom, and again
The gold of newly minted grain.

So Life, by Death the reaper cast
To earth, again shall rise at last;
For 'tis the service of the sod
To render God the things of God.

My grandfather was captivated by the idea that the seed had to die, that is, had to decompose in order for it to produce new life. I think that's what Tabb is getting at in the phrase "so Life, by Death . . ." Though the story Jesus tells and privately explains comments more extensively on the conditions of the soils, it is the dying, decomposing seed that does the work, even as the sower is fast asleep. Even though two of the three soils prove unproductive, the seed always does what it is supposed to do, it dies in the soil and produces new life.

Jesus' parables are bottomless, you never exhaust their meaning, never get to the bottom of them. Perhaps another, new way of looking at this parable is to look past the soils for a moment and focus on the trustworthiness of the seed. It can always be counted on to do what it is supposed to do. It is as if Jesus is telling the Twelve, as he sends them out to scatter the seed for the first time, "Though you will experience all sorts of soils, you can always trust the seed."

♪ *LYRIC NOTE* ♪

You are the soil meant for the seed

Though this parable is bottomless, like all of Jesus' parables, there is a central point around which the teaching turns; what matters is

the condition of the soil, its receptivity, if you will. Some have sug-
gested renaming it "the parable of the soils." The most basic application (though there are others) is that the soils represent people.
The most intimate application is that you are in fact the soil.

14

THE STRANGER

You're still a stranger
Wandering through the wilderness
Still rejected, passed by on the street
Starving, hungry, naked and cold
Pleading for a cup of cold water
Dying all alone
No longer mistaken
For the rebel you truly are
You would still be tearing up temples
Scattering the money of fools
Scandalizing righteous pretenders
Breaking all the rules
No longer blinded
In light I see who you really are
Never doing what is expected
Far beyond the frame of my mind
Caring for the poor and neglected
Washing the feet of the beggar on the street
While the rich men make believe you'll never come
Cowritten with Chuck Beckman

THE STRANGER

The longer you listen, really listen, to the Gospels, the more a mystery begins to grow in your understanding of Jesus. Seeing him, really seeing him through the lens of Scripture, means the old false images are swept away: the gentle Jesus meek and mild, the Jesus as my buddy, the Jesus of the American dream. The mystery is that coming to know him through the Gospels involves a subtle estrangement as well. The Gospels teach us in some sense what he is not, and they often leave us with a stranger, the Stranger.

That is what the Twelve were left with. They ask it over and over again: "Who is this man?" He is not comfortable or predictable, he is not even fully knowable in one sense, at least not in the same way they know each other. How can you *know* someone who is transcendent, whose authority and lordship is absolute? He is not knowable in the sense that other men can be known. Yet there he was, in human flesh, eating, sleeping, weeping, bleeding, and wanting to be known.

It takes a leap to really know him. It requires revelation. You must respond to his Spirit reaching out to you to be known. Peter's Caesarea Philippi confession is one example that revelation, and not perception, allows us to *know* who he is.

The more I gaze on his image in the Gospels, the less of a fan of his I am, less a fan and more a follower, stumbling along with the Twelve, mystified and asking, "Who is this man?"

♪ *LYRIC NOTE* ♪

Washing the feet of the beggar on the street
While the rich men make believe you'll never come

These lines provides the "parting shot" of the song. The Stranger continues to be unrecognized because of the unexpected things he does, like washing feet. He continues to be passed by and rejected because of those he radically identifies with, the poor. As a result, the warning must go out to the rich (you and me) who most often prefer to make believe he has never come.

15

AT HIS FEET

Mark 5:22, 33; 7:25

A fearful, desperate father
Pleads for his dying daughter
He comes, exhausted from sorrow
And falls at His feet
Pale and bleeding, her intent
To touch the fringe of His garment
But, found out, fearfully now, she falls at His feet
    Life and healing in Him meet
    The dark demonic must retreat
    All they had hoped for and more
    They found at His feet
Bruised, bleeding and unclean
He'd lived the life of a bad dream
From the tombs he came trembling
And fell at His feet
With his own voice he was pleading
Another voice, threatened, deceiving
He sought impossible freedom, there at His feet
One rose, one healed of her bleeding
One delivered of thousands of demons
Every one of them found freedom,
There at His feet

Music by Scott Brasher

AT HIS FEET

What do you think? Is this a literary device of Mark? Or is it a
detail from the remembrances of Peter? Or is it both? Or something else altogether? The easy answer is that it is a detail that was
simply a part of the story. The easy answer: it actually happened
this way. Three different people find themselves at the feet of Jesus
and find there everything they could possibly need and more.

This is another example of the need to listen to large blocks of
Scripture instead of focusing on a few verses at a time. In order to
see the structure that holds together the story, you have to look at
a three-chapter block of text: Mark 5:22–7:25.

The story begins with Jesus doing something he continually does
in Mark's Gospel; he is trying to escape from the crowd. In Mark
5:21, Mark tells us he has crossed "again" to the other side of the
lake. Crossing the lake never succeeds in allowing Jesus to escape
the crowds. If you've ever seen the Sea of Galilee, you know that
the lake is small enough that the crowd is able to follow the shoreline
and simply meet Jesus on the other side. Upon landing, probably
at one of the numerous docks that have only been recently discovered, Jesus finds that one of the synagogue leaders, a man
named Jairus, is waiting to meet him. He is the first individual we
will see falling at Jesus' feet. The man's daughter is dying. She's only
twelve years old. Could Jesus please come and heal her?

As Jesus is making his way to the home of the synagogue leader
he is surrounded once again by an enormous crowd. They are
pulling at his clothes or trying to get close enough to touch him.
In that crowd is a woman who is slowly bleeding to death. She's
been dying as long as the little girl has been living. Like so many
others in the crowd she believes that she can simply touch Jesus

and be healed. I call it "magical thinking." Yet this is precisely what happens.

Jesus discovers her hiding in the crowd, and we see the second person falling at his feet. She is afraid and confesses to Jesus everything that has been going through her mind, everything that caused her to break the strict rules of purity and render Jesus unclean by touching him. Within the space of perhaps ten to fifteen minutes, we find two individuals falling at the feet of Jesus.

While Jesus and the woman are speaking, some men come from the house of Jairus. His daughter has died. The delay has been catastrophic. Their comment to Jairus speaks volumes: "Why bother the teacher anymore?" It reveals the level of expectation that everyone had in regards to Jesus. Clearly, he has the power to heal. But no one believed he could raise a person from the dead.

Jesus whispers, "Don't fear . . . only believe."

As they arrive at the house they hear loud mourning. Jesus appears to be confused. Why, he asks, are they making such a commotion? The little girl is not dead, she's only asleep. Jesus always refers to death as sleep, and no one ever understands him. He takes the little girl by the hand and whispers in Aramaic, "Little girl, get up."

The final story happens two chapters later. Jesus and his disciples have traveled on foot some forty miles from Capernaum to the area of Tyre. In Mark 3:8 we already heard of some people from this area coming to hear Jesus speak. Jesus is trying to keep a low profile in this pagan town. Mark tells us he has entered a house, hoping to keep his presence there a secret. But that seems impossible. A woman from the town whose daughter is demon possessed discovers Jesus is there. She is the third person we find falling at Jesus' feet. The miracle happens offstage. Jesus simply tells the woman that when she goes home, she will find her daughter has been delivered. Which is exactly what happened.

What does it mean to fall at Jesus' feet? What does it imply? Perhaps, it begins with exhaustion at having run a long way to find him. Maybe it communicates a sense of submission. But most of all, it is an act of worship, of recognizing the *worth* of Jesus and his ability to triumph over every obstacle, to fulfill every need. His lordship is absolute. It extends over disease, the demonic, and even over death. To fall at his feet is to have arrived in every sense of the word, where everything we long for and everything we need is finally found.

♫ *LYRIC NOTE* ♫

Every one of them found freedom,
There at His feet

While it is interesting to notice the structure and repetition of the phrase "at his feet" in the text, in order to really engage with the text the lyric must do more. It must ask better questions like, "What did all of these people find at the feet of Jesus?" One answer is that they found freedom: freedom from death, disease, and the demonic.

16

YOU WALK
in LONELY PLACES

Mark 6:31; 14:32-42

When they told you of the Baptist
Of what Herod's men had done
You fled into the wilderness
You fled to be alone
And you grieved the world's cruelty
You knew in flesh and bone
The heartache of "mistreated"
And the sorrow of "alone"
Lord, you walked in lonely places
Oh you felt our emptiness
Lord, you walked in lonely places
To know the pain of man
In Gethsemane you struggled
Just to make it through the night
And you called on those who loved you
But weren't ready for the fight
And you pleaded as they slumbered on
You knew in breath and blood
The heartache of "abandoned"
And the suffering of "one"

And in my darkest hours
I call upon your name oh Lord
And you come into the solitude
Of what I cannot face alone
Cause you walk in lonely places
Oh, you felt my emptiness
Lord, you walk in lonely places
To know the pain of man
Cowritten with Sarah Hart

YOU WALK IN LONELY PLACES

We have only the slightest hint of the loneliness of Jesus in Mark
6:31. Upon hearing of the death of his cousin John, he takes the
disciples into the wilderness for what ostensibly is a retreat. "Come
with me, by yourselves, to a quiet place and get some rest," he says.
They had been so overwhelmed by the crowd that they hadn't even
had a chance to eat. The disciples had been out on their first
mission and would no doubt have been exhausted. Away from the
crowd, apparently Jesus would have a chance to mourn the death
of his cousin while the Twelve might have a chance to recover. But
in the end it didn't work out that way. Once again, the crowd saw
them depart by boat and simply followed along the shoreline,
getting there ahead of Jesus. His mourning would have to wait for
another time. His emotional needs would be subsumed by their
hunger for bread.

The other Gospel scene of Jesus' loneliness is of course Gethsemane. He does not really want to be alone, in fact he asks Peter,
James, and John to stay close by. He pleads with them to keep
watch while he prays. They will, all of them, fall asleep at their post,

not once but three times! Jesus' loneliness in the garden is a result of his closest friends' failure to be there for him.

Out of a lengthy time of prayer, Mark only gives us two lines: "Abba, you can do anything, *please* take this cup of suffering away. But not my will but yours be done." Luke speaks of Jesus' sweat becoming blood and of his anguish in the garden. Mark lets us know that it was not the failed, sleeping lookouts who saw the arresting soldiers coming. It was Jesus who saw them. In verse 42 Jesus tells the sleepy disciples, "Look, here comes my betrayer."

Isaiah prophesied the lonely suffering of the Messiah. In Isaiah 53 he foretold that the Messiah would be "a man of sorrows." A man who struggled with senseless death, with the abandonment of his friends, and perhaps most of all with the silence of God.

♫ **LYRIC NOTE** ♫

And in my darkest hours
I call upon your name oh Lord
And you come into the solitude
Of what I cannot face alone

This lyric tries to make the connection between Jesus' experience of loneliness and how it uniquely qualifies him to enter into our experience of being alone. Because he was tempted in every way, just as we are, we can be confident that he understands the temptation that loneliness represents, to give into the thought that we could ever possibly be alone in a world where God's love is always a present reality.

17

IN HIS ARMS

Mark 9:36; 10:16

They came into Capernaum
And settled in the house where they had stayed
Jesus asked if they would say
Why they quarreled on the way
They would not answer
They could not answer
In His arms He held the children
Said whoever welcomes one of these
For the one who is small
Will be greatest of all
And in them you welcome Me
Caught up in another argument
With those who choose to put their wives away
Jesus saw their hearts were numb
To be wed is to be one
They could not sever what God had put together
In His arms He held their children
He would always make the time for them
Though some fathers pretend
For Himself as much as them
He held the children in His arms

IN HIS ARMS

We read twice in Mark that Jesus held the little children in his arms.
If indeed the Gospels only represent .09 percent of his life, then
the actual number would, no doubt, skyrocket. It is clear that Jesus
routinely held children and blessed them. What sort of person
routinely embraces other people's children? What sort of person
takes the time to open the door of their life to children when those
around them have decided that they are clearly too important to
be bothered?

In Mark 9, he has just told them that he is going to be killed
and raised on the third day (v. 31). Mark tells us they were afraid
to ask him about this. What they are not afraid to do, however, is
argue among themselves about which one of them was the greatest
(v. 34). This causes Jesus to take a little child. (I like to think they
were in Peter's house, and it might have been his daughter. One
tradition gives her name as Petronella.) "Whoever welcomes one
of these little ones in my name welcomes me," Jesus says, radically
identifying himself not with the greatest but with those who were
regarded as most insignificant in the culture. It is one of those
parabolic moments, and Peter apparently never forgot it. In response to their selfish argument Jesus embraces a child. "This is
greatness in my kingdom," he says, in effect.

Just a few verses later we see Jesus holding children once more.
Their parents are requesting that Jesus offer a rabbinic blessing that
would've carried with it a prophetic pronouncement, like Jacob
blessing his sons in Genesis 49. In the decades that followed, as the
rabbinic movement took hold (Jesus lived in what we refer to as the
proto-rabbinic period), this would become the solemn duty of the
local rabbi. Jesus' blessing the children here probably would have

been less austere and more tender. It is not yet a formal role but the gracious act of a revered traveling teacher. The Twelve see this as a waste of his time. In contrast, we see Jesus' tender, almost childlike availability. In the disciples' eyes he is too important, because they see themselves as being important. That is why they were arguing about who was greatest.

How dare the disciples take it upon themselves to decide who gets to approach Jesus and who does not? And how dare we do the same thing? This person is not clever enough. This person is not attractive enough or important enough or is a foreigner or poor. But Jesus puts up no walls. He is open to anyone who wants or needs him. He is ready to place his hands on the least and the lost, on the unimportant and the lonely. He is always ready to pronounce the *barocha*, the blessing, that tells us who we are or at least who we might become if we will receive his grace and become as children waiting to be blessed.

♫ LYRIC NOTE ♫

For the one who is small
Will be greatest of all
And in them you welcome Me

Again, this lyric is the key because it sums up the message of the song. Jesus radically identifies with the seemingly small and insignificant children. So complete and radical is his identification that he says we are truly inviting him into the circle of our life whenever we welcome one of them.

18

THE PARADIGM

Mark 10:46-52

He is poor, he is blind
But he will be a paradigm
One of Jesus' greatest finds
There beside the road
Calling out, he has the nerve
To want what he does not deserve
All the beggar's begging for
Is mercy from the Lord
So come all you beggars
Up on your feet, take courage
He's calling to you
Surrender your striving
And find the nerve
To boldly ask for
What you don't deserve
A timeless moment caught in time
The beggar leaves it all behind
Then this perfect paradigm
Calls Jesus by name
Falling down upon his knees
With one request, he wants to see
He could see immediately
When Jesus said, "Go."

THE PARADIGM

He doesn't seem like much, sitting there beside the road to Jerusalem with his coat stretched in front of him to catch the coins he's begging for. He is blind, and because of his blindness he is poor. In Jesus' day he would have been blamed for his blindness. Remember the disciples' earlier question, "Who sinned, this man or his parents, that he was born blind?" (Jn 9:2).

He's heard about Jesus because by this point everyone's heard about Jesus. So he parks himself on the road out of town where he knows Jesus will pass by with a herd of Passover pilgrims on their way to Jerusalem. It's important to recognize that this crowd is not composed only of the followers of Jesus, specifically. Mark says Jesus and the Twelve are "together with" the crowd, which is about to start the steep climb from approximately 1,000 feet below sea level to 2,500 feet above sea level to Jerusalem. As with the children before, the disciples believe the blind man is not worthy of Jesus' time or attention. Their Master is too important, as they are coming to believe that they are too important.

If you are listening to Mark closely, you know Jesus has been looking for followers who are willing to believe without seeing, who will trust him, take his word, and accept who he is without proof. I believe Bartimaeus is the disciple Jesus has been looking for, for three long years now. And he finally finds him, poignantly enough, just a few days before the cross.

There must be a point to Jesus' question, because it is painfully obvious to everyone what Bartimaeus needs. Still he asks, "What do you want me to do for you?" (Mk 10:51). Perhaps he asks because he wants to hear those words from someone, anyone: "I want to see." Perhaps he wants the crowd to hear them or the Twelve. Maybe he knows Bartimaeus needs to say them. Maybe it was for all of these reasons, but say them he does and they hang in the air and echo down the centuries to our ears: "*I want to see!*"

We think we know his name, Bartimaeus. But the truth is we do not. We only know his father's name. Bartimaeus is Aramaic for "son of Timaeus."

Timaeus's nameless son is healed remarkably by one unexpected word from Jesus: "Go!" And Mark tells us he "goes"; that is, he follows Jesus. I'd like to think he accompanied Jesus up the steep ridge all the way to Jerusalem, marveling along the way at all the things he is seeing for the first time with his newly opened eyes.

As remarkable as the story is, perhaps most remarkable is the smallest hint in verse 49 and what it points to. "Have courage," someone in the crowd tells Timaeus's son. Those words point to an ancient message that was spoken directly to Bartimaeus by Isaiah the prophet almost one thousand years earlier. "'Be strong [i.e., "Have courage"] . . . Here is your God. . . . He will save you.' Then the eyes of the blind will be opened" (Is 35:4-5). To Mark's first readers, this word would have been a special encouragement. They too had begun to see the world with new eyes.

♫ LYRIC NOTE ♫

Surrender your striving
And find the nerve
To boldly ask for
What you don't deserve

This lyric sums up what was significant about Bartimaeus's persistent request. He had the nerve to ask for what he did not deserve. This boldness attracted Jesus' attention. In this he becomes a paradigm for us all.

19

IN MEMORY of HER LOVE

Mark 14:1-9

Now at last the time had come
The moment had been waiting
And with her alabaster jar
The woman came to give
It was all she had to give
Pouring out the sweet perfume
Down across His forehead
But some of them began to fume
What this waste was for
It should be spent upon the poor
    Let her be, this is beautiful to Me
    You will have the poor, they'll be with you always
    But can't you see, you'll not always have Me
    The fragrance of her gift
    Will always be remembered
She has done all she could do
Pouring perfume on my body
She has prepared Me for the tomb
Even though she never knew
This is what she came to do

> *What she has done will never fade*
> *From the memory of the gospel*
> *When it is preached around the world*
> *It will be spoken of*
> *In memory of her love*

Cowritten with Sarah Hart

IN MEMORY OF HER LOVE

It would be hard to find a place in the Gospels where so much occurs within the span of so few verses. Here in the opening of Mark 14 we have:

- Jesus sharing the intimacy of a meal fellowship
- the extravagant gift of Mary
- the greatest commendation by Jesus for any disciple, ever
- the beginning of the plot by Judas
- Jesus not simply quoting but breathing the Hebrew Bible

All of this in nine verses!

What is easy to miss, because so much is going on, is Jesus' understanding of what he considers to be beautiful (*kalos*). There seems to be an air of confusion in the room. It has been hanging around Jesus since they left for Jerusalem, just after Peter's great confession in Caesarea Philippi. Jesus is sad and keeps describing in increasing detail precisely what is going to happen to him once they arrive. They are selectively hearing only his references to thrones and their own ideas of what Messiah means: victory, overcoming Rome, and so forth.

In the midst of the confusion Mary presents her extravagant gift, a jar of perfume that was no doubt a family heirloom. After all, this single bottle was worth a year's wages, according to the disciples. The detail is that she breaks the bottle, not just the seal but apparently the neck of the flask, and pours it on Jesus' head. It is extravagant, over the top, and it is her way of letting Jesus know how much she loves him.

Then Jesus says it: "She has done a *beautiful* thing to me." The Greek word is *kalos* and can be translated "good," "noble," "lovely." The later rabbis valued the word so much that they made it into a loan word, simply transliterating it using Hebrew letters.

Of course, that is not the word Jesus actually spoke, since Aramaic was most likely his native language. Perhaps because they were in Judea, he spoke it in Hebrew since it was more commonly spoken in the south. The Bible Society in Israel's Hebrew translation of this term in Mark uses "good deed" (*maasah tov*). The word *tov*, "good," has the characteristic Hebrew depth of meaning, going far beyond our simple idea of goodness. "Beautiful" is a fairly good translation.

So in Jesus' mind, Mary's generous, extravagant, noble, lovely action is "beautiful." Generosity is beautiful to him, as is sacrifice. And tenderness as well is beautiful to Jesus. And finally, beauty to him is legendary in a sense. He says as much when he pronounces a legendary benediction over Mary. He says nothing remotely like this anywhere else or to anyone else. "From now on, wherever the gospel is preached, what she has done will be told as a tribute to her."

What is most memorable is not the offering of the expensive gift but the love that inspired the action. What is most memorable is her love.

♪ LYRIC NOTE ♪

The fragrance of her gift
Will always be remembered

Though it is not the most powerful or poetic line in the song, this lyric sums up both Mary's action and Jesus' memorializing it. It occurs roughly in the middle of the song, which is a good place to encapsulate the content.

20

IS IT ALL OVER NOW?

Mark 16:1-8

Just yesterday in our sorrow,
We tenderly buried the King like a beggar,
Now I despise His light in my eyes,
What has it all been for?

> *Where will I go?*
> *And what will I do?*
> *Is it all over now?*
> *Why did He live?*
> *And what did He die for?*
> *Still I believe somehow, somehow*

Last night, as I slept, through the tears I had wept,
I remembered a curious promise.
What was it He said?
He would rise from the dead
What a desolate hope to cling to.

> *Where will I go?*
> *And what will I do?*
> *Is it all over now?*
> *Why did He live?*
> *And what did He die for?*
> *Still I believe somehow, somehow*

Early this morning, before the sun's dawning,

The women came running in wildly

Trembling with fear, our hope became clear,

As we ran to see if it was true

How could it be?

And what does it mean?

I'd seen His body so lifeless

But now it is gone

And my hope can live on

For Jesus is really risen, He's risen

Cowritten with Brown Bannister

IS IT ALL OVER NOW?

It is hard to recapture the emotional turmoil of Jesus' followers immediately after his death. They had left everything to follow him: home, work, and family. And now it was all simply over. But for the women who were closest to him it was not over; his body still needed to be cared for.

In Jesus' day, two-stage burial was practiced. Step one involved washing and wrapping the corpse. Step two, which occurred a year later, involved washing the bones and placing them in an ossuary or bone box. In spite of what seemed a total failure, utter defeat, the women came to accomplish stage one, to anoint Jesus' corpse. There is absolutely zero expectation among them that he would rise from the dead as he had repeatedly promised. They come to the abandoned quarry, where the tomb is located, to care for a corpse, nothing more. It is all over. The hope of Messiah is as dead as the lifeless body they are expecting to find in the tomb where they had left it before Sabbath began. His life, their life together, was a sad experiment that had failed. Hate won. Death won. The dream was dead.

Mark's brilliance as a writer is nowhere better seen than in the closing of his Gospel. Even in his own day its creative brilliance was unappreciated. At least two different writers tried to "finish" his story properly by adding a few lines, a longer ending, and a shorter one, borrowing bits and pieces from the other Gospels. But the original story, as he first told it, ends with verse 8 and the women afraid, standing outside the empty tomb, perplexed, amazed, and wordless.

The literary mastery of this ending is that it leaves us standing with the women outside the vacant tomb as well. We are forced to cope with the situation exactly as they were. We are forced to believe without seeing the body. We are compelled to trust Jesus' promise without any proof. That was Mark's contribution to the early church, to draw them into the drama of the moment as no other Gospel writer in the decades to follow would do. It was risky and brilliant, and he needs to be deeply appreciated for the literary genius that he was.

♪ LYRIC NOTE ♪

Why did He live?
And what did He die for?
Still I believe somehow, somehow

This lyric works insofar as it communicates the bewilderment of the women at the tomb on resurrection morning. It seeks to put to words and define their feelings of despair and hope mixed together in the moment. It captures that rudimentary hope they held on to in the face of the lack of proof. They saw an empty tomb, which may have been evidence but was no proof.

PART III

LUKE
A World Turned Upside Down

IN ACTS 16:11 there is an abrupt pronoun shift from "they" to "we." What might seem a mundane detail of grammar in fact indicates that the world is quietly being turned upside down, for this is the writer's subtle way of letting us know that he has teamed up with Paul. The writer was a Gentile slave named Luke. We know he was a doctor (Col 4:14) and that most doctors in the first century were slaves. We know too that his name (a shortened form of the name Lucien) also indicates that he was a slave. Slaves were given shortened "hypocoristic" nicknames based on their master's names. So, he has a slave's name and a slave's profession. At that moment when he met Paul on the dock at Troas, his life would never be the same and their friendship and his writings would change our lives forever as well. Their faithful partnership would last to the very end, at a time when Paul's other companions had deserted him. Luke alone would be there (2 Tim 4:11).

If indeed Luke was a slave, it makes sense that he would be warmed to the thought of the world being turned upside down.

Radical reversal and *transvaluation of values* are a couple of the technical/ theological terms for it. But for Luke it is not a matter of systematic theology or even of finding the right word for it. He is hearing it over and over again as he talks to the remaining eyewitnesses of the *event* that was the life and ministry of Jesus.

We tend to forget that in the first century blindness or deafness or being lame was not simply a medical problem to be borne. It was believed to be an indication of sin. So healing and forgiving were intimately linked. In fact, Jesus occasionally healed people by saying, "Your sins are forgiven" (Lk 5:20, 23).

No one seems to be bothered that Jesus can heal, but when he pronounces the forgiveness of sins everyone recognizes that forgiving sins is something only God can do (Lk 5:21).

It is no surprise that when Luke sets himself to the task of writing his two-volume account of the beginnings of the church, a book we know as Luke-Acts, he is preoccupied with the fact that Jesus has turned the world upside down. That he is healing through forgiveness. That those who were insiders, like the Pharisees, are now on the outside, and those who were formally on the outside, tax collectors and sinners like Matthew, are now on the inside. That those who were regarded as poor are now rich with the riches that Jesus has imparted by bringing the kingdom of God into the world. Especially significant for someone like Luke, those who were slaves are being set free!

21

A WORLD TURNED UPSIDE DOWN

Luke 4:18; 7:22; 14:21

Oh Lord, oh my Lord
The time has come for turning
Oh Lord, take this world
And turn it upside down
The lame will walk and the deaf will talk
The time has come for turning
The blind will see and the slave be free
Turn it upside down
The rich man he will wail and moan
The time has come for turning
He'll take the mighty from their thrones
Turn it upside down
The poor will laugh and the beggar will sing
The time has come for turning
He'll feed the hungry with good things
Turn it upside down
Woe to the rich, woe to the free
Woe to the righteous ones who say they see
Blessed are the sufferers, to those who wail and mourn
The world it turning upside down and you can be reborn

Oh Lord, oh my Lord
The time has come for turning
Oh Lord, take this world
And turn it upside down
Cowritten with Scott Brasher and Joan Brasher

♫ LYRIC NOTE ♫

The lyric is a shopping list of the radical reversal Luke is so fond
of; the lame will walk, the deaf talk, the blind receive their sight,
and (of particular interest to Luke) those who were enslaved will
be set free. But the reversal goes both ways. The rich will wail and
moan and be unseated from their thrones. This theme was first
sung by Jesus' mother, Mary, in chapter 1. It is a song that is sus-
tained throughout the entire Gospel.

22

WHAT SORT of SONG?

Luke 1:46-55

What sort of song do you sing when an angel
Has said a new world will be born in you?
That you should not fear now because you are favored
How do you believe unbelievable news?
That you'll bear His baby, the Son of the Most High
That you'll name Him Jesus, oh how to reply?
Oh what sort of song do you sing?
What sort of song do you sing?
My soul praises the Lord and my spirit rejoices in God, my Savior
For He's been mindful of the humble estate of His servant
From now on all generations will call me "blessed"
For the Mighty One had done great things in me
What sort of song can you possibly sing
When impossible prophecies come to your life?
How do you make music when someday this burden
Will give birth to sorrow and cut like a knife?
This beautiful baby will be born to die
To offer salvation, oh how to reply?
Oh what sort of song do you sing?
What sort of song do you sing?
His great mercy reaches out to all generations

> *His strong and mighty arm has scattered the vain and the proud*
> *He's brought down mighty princes, but lifted up the lowly*
> *And filled the hungry with good things*
> *Because of His covenant love*

WHAT SORT OF SONG?

One of the great debts we owe to Luke is his preservation of the songs that were sung in response to the Spirit moving at the coming of Jesus. Singing in the Bible is almost always prophetic in character. In the songs of Mary and Simeon we hear the prophetic spirit, which had been silent for 350 years, come to life once more. Most especially we are drawn to the very first of those songs, sung by Mary the mother of Jesus.

Her lyric raises the question, How do you respond to this kind of unheard-of situation? What do you say? What words do you piece together in response to an angel who appears, telling you that you're going to give birth to the Savior of the world? That is Mary's dilemma. And the truth is—there are no words. And that is why she sings.

The song she sings reveals a heart that has been saturated in the Scripture. Mary does not simply quote passages from the Hebrew Bible as she sings. No, like her son, Mary breathes biblical images. They come out naturally as a part of her song. She is rejoicing as she sings that a long-forgotten promise has now been acted upon by the Lord and she is a part of making that promise come true. We see in Mary an immediate surrender of all that she is, all her hopes, all her dreams, even her own body, to the will of the One who is making this ancient promise come true.

♪ *LYRIC NOTE* ♪

What sort of song can you possibly sing
When impossible prophecies come to your life?

This line, positioned in the middle of the song, restates the question the lyric is based on. This song is sung in a sense by Mary herself. The chorus is the Magnificat, the song she sings in Luke. I like combining it with a series of questions, also from her point of view.

23

A KING in
a CATTLE TROUGH

Luke 2:1-20

How do you capture the accents of angels?
How do you put words to the taste of their light?
You cannot describe how their words burn right through you
How you became dizzy with heart-pounding fright
In the midst of your fear how they sang you a song
To the glory of God Most High
How all of the sudden, that when they departed
That they left a hole in the sky
How do you worship a king in a cattle trough?
When you cannot bow any lower than He?
And what kind of gift to give Someone with nothing?
In humiliating humility
Wrapped up in rags, what a heart-breaking sign
Yet on His sweet face what delight
The darkness that prowls here cannot comprehend
This impossibly bright point of light
So everyone listened in awe and amazement
To all we'd been told 'bout this beautiful boy
But Mary His mother, she wordlessly wondered
And pondered her treasure of joy

> *Who could conceive how the Savior was born*
> *In a place only fit for the cattle to feed*
> *His poverty made Him our perfect Provision*
> *The one hope for our every need*

A KING IN A CATTLE TROUGH

Luke is not interested in magi, in gold and royal gifts. He is captivated by humble shepherds and an infant sleeping in a cattle trough, which might have been nothing more than a hole carved out in the cold stone floor. In his Gospel, apart from Jesus' mother, the revelation of Jesus' birth is first spoken to outsiders, the shepherds. Like most of the other main characters in Luke's Gospel, the shepherds were marginalized in the first century; they were later barred by a rabbinic mandate from testifying in a court of law. They must have been considered untrustworthy, hardly worthy of being the first witnesses to the birth of the Messiah.

It appears to be spring because they are keeping a watch all night in the fields, most likely due to the fact that springtime is when lambs are generally born. Another tradition teaches that, owing to the fact that they were so close to Jerusalem and the temple, the sheep they were caring for were destined to be sacrificed and had to be constantly watched to make sure they remained spotless.

The time of year and the reason for the shepherds being in the field all night are debatable. But without question, these humble men are the first worshipers of Jesus, the first to approach him, having been informed by the angels as to exactly who he is—a king in a cattle trough!

Of all the Gospel writers, Luke seems to appreciate this disconnect the most. Mary and Zechariah have sung their songs. The angels too have sung or spoken their lyrical praise of Jesus to the shepherds, as Simeon will do in just a few verses. In a year or two, when the magi finally find him, Matthew tells us they will worship the holy toddler. But what about the shepherds?

Luke tells us they hurried off to find Jesus (v. 16) and that after they had seen him they left "glorifying and praising God for all that they had seen" (v. 20). But there is no word of what took place in the darkness of the stable. Luke leaves us to assume that they adored the baby in some fashion, and it's a safe assumption. Yet still the question stands: How did the first witnesses of the incarnation respond? Perhaps Luke did not think to ask Mary the question as he interviewed her for his Gospel. Perhaps she did not remember, so caught up was she in her own adoration. So the question forever remains unanswered and unanswerable.

♫ **LYRIC NOTE** ♫

His poverty made Him our perfect Provision
The one hope for our every need

While not my favorite ("darkness that prowls here," I like best), this line seeks to answer the question the song is asking. This song comes from the shepherds, and the question it asks echoes Mary's question in the previous song. What words, what melody could hope to capture all the paradoxical emotions that are swirling around that stone trough? Hope and despair, kingship and poverty.

24

SIMEON'S SONG

Luke 2:25-35

An old man in the temple
Waiting in the court
Waiting for the answer to a promise
And all at once he sees them
In the morning sunshine
A couple coming carrying a baby
    Now that I've held Him in my arms
    My life can come to an end
    Let your servant now depart in peace
    I've seen your salvation
    He's the light of the Gentiles
    And the glory of His people Israel
Mary and the baby come
And in her hand five shekels
The price to redeem her baby boy
The baby softly cooing
Nestled in her arms
Simeon takes the boy and starts to sing
    And now's the time to take Him in your arms
    Your life will never come to an end
    He's the only way that you'll find peace

> *He'll give you salvation*
> *He's the light of the Gentiles*
> *And the glory of His people Israel*

SIMEON'S SONG

He stands there, his eyes dim, his frame feeble. We think of him as a remarkably old man, his vitality gone. The truth is the text does not indicate how old Simeon actually was. We are told Anna had been a widow for eighty-four years. We assume he is old due to the promises he receives. They are the kind of promises that are made to old men.

We see him sometimes in our imaginations, late at night as he lies aching in bed wondering if he really heard that luminous promise that he would not die until the coming of the Messiah. Even the morning that it came true, did he wonder to himself if it had all been a dream?

Like so many other characters associated with the birth of Jesus early in Luke's Gospel, Simeon's response is a song. His life can come to an end because now everything he hoped for has come true. And so, he sings. The baby he holds in his arms is not only the fulfillment of the promise to him. He is the hope of the Gentiles, a promise kept from the very beginning (Gen 3:15). And so he sings, because only a lyrical response can make sense out of a situation that leaves you otherwise speechless!

♫ LYRIC NOTE ♫

> *He's the light of the Gentiles*
> *And the glory of His people Israel*

It is a subtle thing you would hardly notice, but this line is sung by two voices in the song. First by Simeon in the process of simply recounting the story. The second time it is sung by the singer (whoever he or she or they might be!) and serves as an invitation to enter into Simeon's experience of realizing who Jesus is and what he means. He is Light (a theme John's Gospel loves to talk about), and he is glory.

25

A LITTLE BOY LOST

Luke 2:41-51

THAT MARY WAS ONE of Luke's eyewitnesses can almost be
taken for granted. A reliable tradition says Luke wrote his Gospel
in the city of Ephesus, and there is every indication that Mary was
living with the disciple John in that same city. Luke's Gospel knows
what Mary is thinking and feeling. Luke tells stories that only Mary
could have told and from her point of view. She is one of his
sources. The mother of Jesus!

One story that could have only come from her is the single incident we have from the childhood of Jesus. We are told he is only
twelve years old. Luke records that Mary and Joseph and Jesus
make their way to Jerusalem. It is a journey Jesus will make three
and sometimes four times every year, spending as much as three
months of each year going back and forth to Jerusalem. Apparently,
his parents did the same as well.

Imagine being entrusted with raising the Messiah only to lose
him for three days! And yet that is exactly what happens. When
they finally find Jesus after what must have been a frantic search,
he seems to be confused by the fact that they are so upset. The little
boy does not understand why they looked everywhere for him. In
his mind, they should've come straight to the temple.

We read tantalizing stories like this in the Gospels and long for more detail from the extraordinary life of this little boy. What was it like for him to grow up? Just how ordinary was his childhood? Yet this story from Luke is the only precious window we have.

In Luke's account Jesus is both ordinary and exceptional. He is twelve and would have been regarded as an adult. There are no teenagers in Judaism. You're a boy or a man. And so, the image of the twelve-year-old in the temple talking to the rabbis and asking them questions is a relatively ordinary picture. Although it is sometimes presented as out of the ordinary, as proof of his young genius, that the teachers would be asking the twelve-year-old Jesus questions is ordinary as well. That is simply how they teach. What is extraordinary is that the rabbis are "astounded" at his understanding and his answers.

The story ends with a close-up of Mary. She is treasuring all these things and pondering them in her heart. This will no doubt be an experience she will have over and over again in the eighteen or so years she has left with Jesus. Ordinary moments punctuated by extraordinary experiences that are simply beyond her imagination.

26

THE BRIDGE

Luke 10:25-37

There was a legal-minded man
Intellectually inclined
But the facts just seemed to pile up
And fester in his mind
So he asked the twisted question
"What am I supposed to do?"
His heart said he should love
But his mind still wondered "who?"
    From the head to the heart
    From the heart to the mind
    The Truth must make a journey
    If we ever hope to find
    You can see it as a bridge
    On a narrow winding road
    But the fact is Truth must travel
    If it ever will be told
The answer came concealed
In the story Jesus told
Of a lonely, outcast traveler
Upon a dangerous road
The men with all answers

> *Left the wounded man to die*
> *While the lonely clueless stranger*
> *Refused to pass him by*
> *The answer's not an answer*
> *If it's for the mind alone*
> *It's the orchard in the apple seed*
> *It's the seed that must be sown*
> *It has to do with loving*
> *And giving all you have to give*
> *And only those who cross the bridge*
> *Can ever hope to live*

THE BRIDGE

We take for granted that Jesus entered a fallen world. Rarely do we stop to think about the nature of that fallenness. Jesus' world is fragmented. Judaism is not one entity in Jesus' time. A well-known Jewish scholar refers to the "Judaisms" of the first century. But that fragmentation wasn't simply social or religious. It makes its way down to each individual heart and mind. The truth is we are, all of us, fragmented.

This is seen in the way we approach Scripture. Rarely do we embrace God's Word with all our hearts and all our minds, as Deuteronomy 6:5 encourages us to do. Some of us embrace Scripture with our minds. We lean toward theology, and we look for answers. And there is nothing wrong with that except that it is ultimately incomplete. Some of us come to the Scriptures with our hearts in the forefront. We read devotionally. We are not looking for answers as much as a genuine experience. And likewise, there's nothing wrong with this either. But the Bible speaks to the whole person, all of the heart as well as the mind. It seeks to recapture them both by means of the imagination.

Jesus reaches out to this fragmentation in his teaching. He does not simply teach didactic theological truth. That is, he is not simply appealing to the minds of his listeners. Neither does he simply utter devotions that would primarily touch the hearts of his listeners. No, Jesus engages the whole person. The heart as well as the mind. And this is seen most clearly in his parables.

Luke contains more parables than any other Gospel. In his parables Jesus seeks to cross a bridge between the heart and the mind: the imagination. In one scene a teacher of the law comes to Jesus asking a question. Notice Jesus answers the lawyer's question not with a lesson but with a story. The lawyer must listen fully, with all his heart and mind, or he will not receive the lesson. "He who has ears to hear" is Jesus' way of saying, "If you don't engage with the story, you're not going to get it."

♫ LYRIC NOTE ♫

From the head to the heart
From the heart to the mind
The Truth must make a journey

These lines succinctly state the fact that *truth must travel* across the bridge of the imagination, which lies between the head and the heart. That is the function of the parables of Jesus. They demand engagement of both the heart and the mind.

27

A BREATH of a PRAYER

Luke 11:1-4

It takes a single breath to say
Lord have mercy, Christ have mercy
A breath of a prayer to say
Lord have mercy, Christ have mercy
Lord Jesus, Son of God
Have mercy on me, a sinner
Father, hallowed be Your Name
Your kingdom come
Give unto us each day
Our daily bread
Forgive us as we forgive
All those who sin against us
And lead us not into temptation
Cowritten with Scott Roley

A BREATH OF A PRAYER

In the Judaism of Jesus' time the day was punctuated with prayer three times a day. Prayer, fasting, and giving to the poor were not optional. They were regarded as the pillars of the faith, and everyone was expected to be observant. (Jesus added one innovation to all three, that they be done in secret [Mt 6:1-18].) So the question was not do we pray, or even especially when do we pray, but rather *how* to pray? Apparently John the Baptist had taught his followers about prayer. In Luke 11:1 Jesus' disciples ask that he do the same thing for them.

Interpreters of Luke's Gospel have often been puzzled by the fact that even though Jesus is seen at prayer at every important turning point, when Jesus finally prays what has become to be known as the Lord's Prayer, Luke gives us roughly half its length. This misunderstanding of Luke's intentions is based on the idea that the longer the prayer is, the better. That somehow Luke's short form of Jesus' prayer is inferior to the longer version (Mt 6:9-13) of the other Gospels. But to truly understand the nature of prayer is to see that more is not necessarily better. In fact more often than not, the shorter the prayer, the more to the point it is.

And so in the Gospel of Luke when his disciples asked to be instructed in prayer as John the Baptist had apparently instructed his own disciples, Jesus gives them an example that can be spoken with a single breath. Perhaps the shorter form is the more preferable after all.

♪ *LYRIC NOTE* ♪

It takes a single breath to say
Lord have mercy, Christ have mercy

This is a very simple song. It is meant to provide a setting for the words of the Lord's Prayer. The opening line, however, makes an additional point that implies a hundred things about Jesus' exemplary prayer, especially Luke's shorter version. It literally can be said with a single breath, and moreover it is stark in its simplicity while at the same time still being complete.

28

HOW MUCH MORE a SERVANT COULD HE BE?

Luke 22:14-30

On this their final night, they bicker and they fight
Still they are slaves to men, but not yet slaves to Christ
He would give up on words, too tired to speak
So He took up the towel and washed their filthy feet
    The arguments just melt away
    And there was nothing more that they could say
    A wordless lesson that would set them free
    Tell me, how much more a servant could He be?
He took a loaf of bread, He broke it and He said
Take this My body and remember Me
He took the final cup and as He raised it up
This covenant is new, My blood poured out for you
The arguments just melt away
And there was nothing more that they could say
A wordless lesson that would set them free
Tell me, how much more a servant could He be?
He is the slave who always serves Himself
And makes of Himself the final meal
Lived out in flesh so we could see
Tell me, how much more a servant could He be?

He is the wine and bread, too much to comprehend
He leads us from His knees and serves us as a friend
In time they'd finally hear the message made so clear
Who is the greatest One? It is God's Servant Son
Cowritten with Scott Roley

HOW MUCH MORE A SERVANT COULD HE BE?

Luke omits the foot washing, as do all the Synoptics, yet in a sense he does not. Himself a slave, Luke's heart would have resonated with Jesus performing the act of the lowliest slave by washing the disciples' feet. But, like the others, he can't bring himself to tell the humiliating story. Only John, decades later, will be able to tell it.

But Luke gives us the setting, the reason for the foot washing, when no other Gospel writer does. He tells us that after the supper an argument broke out over who was the greatest. He was responding to this argument when John tells us Jesus got up from the meal and proceeded to wash their feet. They argue about who is the greatest, and Jesus responds by demonstrating what true greatness really is—servanthood. After the meal and the foot washing it appears they never argued about who was greatest again.

Luke gives us one more piece of evidence for what had happened, for the pitiful story he cannot bring himself to tell. In verse 27, in the discussion about true greatness that must have followed the washing of the disciples' feet, he records that Jesus said, "I am among you as the one who serves." Those are the words of the person who had just washed their feet.

Toward the end of the first century, as the rabbinic movement was gaining momentum, it was noticed that some disciples were becoming too admiring of their rabbis. In response a mandate was issued: "Every task that a slave does for his master will a disciple do for his teacher, except one. He shall not loosen the thong of his sandal." Loosening the sandal was regarded as too demeaning. This might lie behind John the Baptist's statement in Luke 3:16, where he proclaims that he is not even worthy to loosen Jesus' sandal.

Given all that, how much greater is the humility of the One who, more than loosening the sandal, is willing to wash his disciples' feet. Next to the cross itself, it is the kairotic act of the servanthood of Jesus. And only Luke gives us the fingerprints.

♫ *LYRIC NOTE* ♫

Tell me, how much more a servant could He be?

Basing a song on a question often says more than writing a lyric filled with answers. Questions, like parables, force the listener to engage or not.

29

THE PAIN and
PERSISTENCE of DOUBT

Luke 24:1-12

In the light of the dawn, at the dawn of the day
As a night that seemed endless was done
In emptiness, in hopelessness
To care for a corpse, they come
In the dim morning light, they thought they just might
Have caught a glimpse of a stone rolled away
In fear they bow, not knowing how
They could hear an angel say

   Why search for the living here among the dead?
   Can't you see that He's simply not here?
   Why can you not figure out
   What His words were all about?
   When will you let go of the pain
   And persistence of doubt?

In heart-pounding hope they ran back from the tomb
To tell the impossible truth
Did they succumb to delirium?
And believe unbelievable news?
In our own world and in our own way
We live like this mystery's not true

> *But if we'd take care and defy the despair*
> *In our own ears the words might ring true*
> Music by Scott Brasher

THE PAIN AND PERSISTENCE OF DOUBT

Delirium (*lēros*) is the medical term that Luke uses to describe the women. It does not say the women were delirious but that the eleven apostles thought they were. To the apostles these were simply emotional women caught up in the moment of their sorrow, their grief. After all, there is no way it could be true! Delirium implies that the women's eyes were playing tricks on them based on a false expectation. That perhaps they expected Jesus might really rise from the dead. But it is clear from the text (and this cannot be overstated) they had absolutely no expectation of his resurrection. They had come to care for a corpse. Even after they'd seen that the stone had been removed, no one jumps to the conclusion that Jesus has been raised from the dead. They only assume that someone has stolen the body. There was no expectation, hence no delirium.

The stories that surfaced following the resurrection of Jesus of Nazareth give evidence of the persistence of doubt. In spite of his repeated promises that he would be raised from the dead, despite the evidence of the stone rolled away and the empty tomb, his first followers held on to their doubt. Confronting their pernicious doubt is the angelic question, "Why are you looking for the living among the dead?" After all, angels are always asking questions that indicate the person they are talking to has no real grasp of the situation.

The story of the women outside the tomb is our story as well. Again and again as we follow Jesus we come to the realization of what the empty tomb really means. It's not as if we accept it once and move on, squeezing out all the meaning once and for all. And that means Luke means for us to hear in our own ears the question asked by the angel. Why do we so often search for the living among the dead? Why do we so often search in the wrong place with our faithless expectations? Why do we keep on expecting to find lifelessness in a place where again and again Jesus has promised new life?

♩ LYRIC NOTE ♩

To care for a corpse, they come

This brief line expresses the notion of *zero expectation*. That is why it is central to the song. The women are not coming to the tomb to see if what Jesus promised had happened, after all. They are carrying spices to anoint a dead body, to care for a corpse.

30

SEVEN ENDLESS MILES

Luke 24:13-35

Forlorn footsteps follow
A pathway of denial
The pathway to Emmaus
Down seven endless miles
Forsaken hopeless followers
So faithlessly assume
There's no One left to follow
Hope was buried in the tomb
As they discuss and argue
And want to disagree
Before where only two were
Now suddenly there's three
What things were you discussing
Could you explain to me?
He asked as He stepped out
Beyond the edge of mystery
But their pain and disappointment
Was more than they could tell
For they had hoped He was the One
To rescue Israel
   How foolish of heart

How slow to believe
Come be reconciled
On these seven endless miles
Faith will see beyond
The mystery's disguise
The miracle of broken bread
Can open up your eyes

SEVEN ENDLESS MILES

Take care to listen closely to the words of the dejected disciples. They had given up any hope that something had happened in Jerusalem. Now making their way back down to the city of Emmaus, "We had hoped," they said. In spite of the fact that they have heard the miraculous message from the women that Jesus had been raised from the dead, they cannot find it within themselves to believe. Still their doubt persists, persists to the degree that they are walking away from the scene of the crime. They had given up the notion of waiting Jesus out to see if it could possibly be true. They are going home. It's over.

Even as they are in the process of leaving the scene, Jesus' kindness reaches out in an interesting and creative way. His love will not let them go. All of a sudden he's walking along the road with them. He is able to somehow cloak his appearance. Though they are his disciples and had been in his presence, they do not recognize Jesus. He walks along with them, engages their doubt, and begins to teach them a significant lesson.

Jesus unpacks for them all the promises of the Hebrew Bible regarding the Messiah, promises that they should have known. But even the lesson seems unable to reach through the persistence of their doubt. At the meal, upon the breaking of the bread, whatever had kept them from recognizing him is lifted and they recognize the risen Lord.

Luke is careful to say it was the moment when Jesus broke the bread that their eyes were opened and they recognized him. The breaking of bread was, in effect, a miracle Jesus used to cure the particular blindness of their disbelief.

The breaking of bread . . . it is a miracle that occurs thousands of times a day all over this tired globe. At the very moment when most of us are moving in the opposite direction, Jesus calls us back, turns us around, and opens our eyes at that miraculous moment when the bread is broken.

♫ *LYRIC NOTE* ♫

Forlorn footsteps follow
A pathway of denial

Here again the opening verses serve to set the tone for the whole lyric. The story is about a walk that is taking two of Jesus' followers in the opposite direction from the miracle of resurrection and Jerusalem. The story we know as the "Road to Emmaus" should be known as the "Road *Away* from Jerusalem."

PART IV

JOHN
The Misunderstood Messiah

HIS EYES ARE GROWING DIM. He walks with a shuffle. Sometimes he needs help getting up from his chair. After all, he is almost one hundred years old! To the average citizen of Ephesus, he is simply a remarkably old man, but to those in the rapidly growing church in Ephesus he is the last living disciple of Jesus of Nazareth: John the Elder.

I imaging seeing him tottering down one of the alleyways of the ancient city of Ephesus. There is one story of him running out of one of the baths yelling that the roof might fall in because a heretic named Cerinthus had just entered the building. Perhaps age has robbed him of his sense of decorum along with his teeth and most of his hair.

The one thing that remains untouched by the years is his youthful imagination. Whenever he launches into one of his myriad stories, he assumes the energy of a teenager. He has told them a thousand times.

He knows the stories that cause the crowd to gasp or roll their eyes or even to laugh. Like the one about the man born blind who innocently asks the angry Pharisees, who keep asking questions about Jesus, if they too want to become his followers. It's a funny story, and people have been laughing at it for two thousand years. He knows which stories work, which ones people will respond to, and which ones need some explaining. And so, unique to his Gospel, John's constant whispering is supplying the information he has come to realize his listeners need to fully understand the story.

Peter has been dead for over thirty years. The Eleven are all gone. Once the Lord takes John, none of them will be left. He is revered and listened to as perhaps none of Jesus' other disciples ever have been.

31

COME and SEE

John 1:39

Come and see, come follow me
Back to the place where He's staying
He'll not mind, for there you will find
All that your faith has been waiting
Come see the Way, the Truth, and the Life
Come see the Light that is living
Come now and see how the Truth sets you free
For a lifetime of loving and giving
Come and see, come follow me
On a road where believing is seeing
There's work to do and words of truth
To find in your heart for the speaking
Come see the Servant who's also a King
See how He kneels by the table
Come now and see how abundant and free
To become the slave of the Savior
Come and see, come follow me
To a garden He's watered with weeping
Though shadows cling the angels will sing
Of the promise He's painfully keeping
Come see a hill that is shaped like a skull

> *See on the cross He is reeling*
>
> *He will provide from the wound in His side*
>
> *Both water and blood for our healing*
>
> *Come and see, follow me*
>
> *To the writer of parable pages*
>
> *That fiery child, so angry and wild*
>
> *Now is ink-fingered and aged*
>
> *Come see the place where he laid down and died*
>
> *After long ages of serving*
>
> *A lifetime to learn what he could not have earned*
>
> *It was never about being worthy.*
>
> Cowritten with Jon Reddick

COME AND SEE

The second thing John records hearing Jesus say (the first was "What are you looking for?") was "Come and see." He had no way of knowing that the words of that first invitation would shape his life. He spent the next eighty or so years issuing the same invitation through his preaching and teaching and most especially his most elegant Gospel.

It began for John with that first invitation to come and see where Jesus was staying (Jn 1:39). We are left to wonder exactly where Jesus was staying, but that is the wrong question (though it is still a good question). What matters is the remarkable openness of Jesus and his welcoming response to the prospective disciples. John will remember that they spent the rest of the day with him.

After that initial time together came the call to follow, to go on the road with Jesus, where believing would be seeing. John would learn as much from Jesus' humble acts of servanthood as he would his luminous words. His actions would become the blueprint for John's own long life of radical servanthood.

Then there was that most awful of moments, of which John was an eyewitness (Jn 19:23, 26). There is no word of any of the other disciples being there. Perhaps John felt someone needed to stay with the women, one of whom was his own mother, Salome. He witnessed the mysterious detail of the blood and water leaking from the wound in Jesus' side.

Finally, seven decades later, we see John, no longer the youthful follower but the aged saint, the leader of seven churches located on a postal road in the Roman province of Asia. He can tell stories no one else knows. He is the last living disciple. Peter has been dead for thirty years. It is difficult to imagine the awe he would have inspired simply by his presence.

♪ *LYRIC NOTE* ♪

Come follow me

This lyric takes Jesus' original response to the disciples' first question, "Rabbi, where are you staying?" and applies it to the rest of his ministry. That simple phrase becomes something of a bookmark or an invitation to "see" more scenes from Jesus' life. The song is told from the standpoint of the life and experience of John, without him being the central character.

32

The BREAD,
the LIGHT, the LIFE

John 6:35; 9:1-41; 11:52

Jesus walked into the hills
The One who said, "I am the bread"
There He blessed five loaves of barley
And there the thousands humbly fed
A man was born in darkness
The blame they could not qualify
The One who said, "I am the Light"
Restored the sight to blinded eyes
　He was the broken bread of life
　　Of all the world, the Light was He
　In Him Life had come alive
　　The deaf and blind could hear and see
Lazarus His friend had died
"I am the Life," had Jesus said
Standing there outside the tomb
He spoke the words that raised the dead

THE BREAD, THE LIGHT, THE LIFE

He had learned directly from Jesus the art of understanding life
parabolically. In fact, one wonders if John had not become

convinced that this was the only way to truly understand anything of real significance. It was how Jesus understood and explained the kingdom of God, service to God, prayer, obedience, Jesus' own sacrifice. He had used parables to help the youthful John and his companions grasp the true meaning of all of these and more. And now the elderly John, the revered leader of the church in Ephesus, decided that he would create his own parables to explain what he considered to be of the utmost significance—the life of Jesus.

Even the order is significant; John begins with the parable of Jesus as the bread of life. This is associated with the feeding of the five thousand. The action of Jesus in providing bread for the multitude is a parable in and of itself (Jn 6:1-15). But then, a few verses later, Jesus says plainly, "I am the bread of life" (v. 35). The truth of who Jesus is as the bread was revealed in the parabolic story of the feeding of the five thousand.

Next comes the parabolic story of the healing of the blind man (Jn 9). Earlier, in John 8:12, after the encounter with the woman taken in adultery, Jesus had made the pronouncement that he was the light of the world. Now John tells the parabolic story, which covers an entire chapter, of the healing of the man born blind. Jesus, who is the bread, had fed the multitude. Now Jesus, who is the light, will restore the sight to a blind man. The actual story works like a parable to reveal the truth about who Jesus really is.

Finally, in ascending order, comes the story of the raising of Lazarus. First, the simple bread, next the more miraculous provision of healing the blind, and now finally the miracle of the restoration of life, of resurrection.

As Jesus is making his way to the scene, Martha intercepts him just outside of town. His promise of resurrection ("Your brother will rise again" [Jn 11:23]) she apparently takes as a simple word of comfort. Then Jesus speaks the words that will be parabolically demonstrated beside Lazarus's tomb: "I am the resurrection and the life" (v. 25). He is preparing her—and us—for the moment that is about to come, for the revelation via parabolic act.

After a brief interaction with Martha's sister, Jesus stands beside the sealed tomb. Inside is the wrapped and lifeless body of his beloved friend. There are no histrionics. No lightning bolts from his fingertips. He simply calls for his friend to come out. And come out he does.

Bread, light, life . . . Those things we need the most to survive and thrive (along with water, which Jesus also provides [Jn 4:10; 7:38]) are parables of who *he* is. Our need of them are parabolic pointers to the reality of who *he* is.

♫ LYRIC NOTE ♫

He was the broken bread of life
Of all the world, the Light was He
In Him Life had come alive

The chorus recaps the three elements of the Johannine parable that is Jesus' life: bread, light, and life. It is certain that this structure is intentional in John's Gospel due to the fact that they are each connected to one of the "I AM" sayings. While it is safe to say this structure was "Spirit breathed," I can't help but believe that it is also a product of decades of John's preaching and teaching his hungry followers. They were categories of Jesus that became John's basis for understanding his Savior and friend.

33

THE ONE WHO WAS SENT

John 5:24; 7:16; 17:3; 8:23; 20:21

Like Moses He would speak the words of God
He would be misunderstood, considered a fraud
When they asked Him where He came from
He would answer
They would hear His words to their astonishment
He had not come to judge or to condemn them
To do the Father's will
He was sent

   He is the One who was sent by the Father
   He is the One who acted out of love
   He is the One who was led by the Spirit
   He is the One who was sent from above

While we have the light of day we speak His word
The night is coming soon when no one can work
When they asked Him where He came from
He would answer
They would hear His words to their astonishment
He had not come to judge or to condemn them
To do the Father's will
He was sent
It was never His will

> *To leave us alone*
> *For He is faithful and true*
> *The One who was sent is calling us to go*
> *As the Father has sent me, so I am sending you*
> Cowritten with Scott Roley

THE ONE WHO WAS SENT

Just who does Jesus think he is? I love that question, if for no other reason than the hubris behind it. His identity in John's Gospel is tied to this favorite circumlocution for his Father, "the one who sent me." Jesus uses it almost thirty times. If you ask him who he thinks he is, from the pages of John's Gospel Jesus will unquestionably answer, "I am the one who was sent."

His identity as the "sent one" connects Jesus to the prophecy of Deuteronomy 18 and the prophet Moses. Like Moses, Jesus is sent. Also like Moses, Jesus only speaks the words the Father gives him to speak. Moses speaks of the promise of manna. Jesus promises to give himself as the living bread. Moses strikes the rock and provides water in the wilderness. Jesus promises to be the source of living water. The parallels are impossible to ignore.

Unlike Moses, Jesus' identity as the sent one implies where he was sent from. It is called the "ascending-descending" motif in John's Gospel. He is the one who descended from heaven (like the manna) and who will be ascending to heaven (Jn 3:13).

In one of the pivotal moments in John's Gospel, Jesus, the sent one, passes on that same identity to the eleven apostles. In John 20:21, just before imparting the Spirit by means of his breath, Jesus tells the Eleven, "As the Father sent me, I also send you." They will speak his words and do his work, not their words or work.

♪ LYRIC NOTE ♪

The One who was sent is calling us to go
As the Father has sent me, so I am sending you

The closing line of the lyric expresses the moment the disciples are granted the new identity that was so central to Jesus in John's Gospel. His Father is the one who sent him. He is the one who was sent. And now, at the close of his earthly ministry, Jesus imparts the dimensions of that identity to the disciples and to us.

34

HOW CAN THESE THINGS BE?

John 3:1-13

Ancient footsteps in the gloom
An open door, a lighted room
A youthful rabbi, an elderly man
Who'd give it all just to understand
 How could these things be?
 How can I accept this mystery?
 Am I being healed of this blindness
 Of believing that I could see?
He clings to his own righteousness
Of being good to be blessed
But Jesus speaks of a healing wind
The fact of being born again
As Moses lifted up the snake
In the wilderness the curse to break
So Jesus must be lifted high
To give us life He must die
So He will pay our penalty
To make us whole and to set us free

HOW CAN THESE THINGS BE?

We can't help but love Nicodemus; the powerful Jew with the pagan name comes to Jesus representing a broken Judaism. He is a Pharisee, a member of the Sanhedrin. He is unique in that he sees that he does not see; he understands that he does not understand.

In my mind's eye I see the scene as a fifteenth-century painting, like Rembrandt, painted in light and shadow; it's a night scene, lit by olive oil lamps. He is a poster child for the first-century fragmentation of Judaism. Though a powerful member of what amounts to the Supreme Court, he is powerless to fully understand the complexities of someone like Jesus. He must have it explained to him or perhaps *revealed* to him. He is drawn to Jesus and is obviously open to hearing what he has to say.

Later, in John 7, he appears again at a gathering of Jewish leaders, the chief priests and Pharisees, who have come together to discuss what to do about Jesus. The burly Benjamite temple guards have come back empty-handed, having been sent to arrest Jesus. "No one ever spoke the way this man speaks" is all they can stammer. Amid the heated accusations Nicodemus speaks up on behalf of Jesus. He makes a legal point that the Torah does not condemn someone until they have had a chance to speak for themselves. For making this simple point of law Nicodemus is attacked and accused of being a follower of Jesus, which as far as we know, he is not quite yet.

Roughly three years later Nicodemus appears in John's Gospel once again, alongside Joseph of Arimathea. They have come to "boldly" claim the body of Jesus. While Nicodemus's discipleship in John 7 may be up for grabs, here in chapter 19 he is undoubtedly a committed follower.

All that talk about wind and Spirit and birth all those years ago during Passover in Jerusalem with Jesus, his invitation to the old man to come into the light, all those seeds finally took root in Nicodemus's heart and mind. The answer to that first question he muttered in confusion all those years ago, "How can these things be?" Nicodemus finally found.

♫ *LYRIC NOTE* ♫

Am I being healed of this blindness .
Of believing that I could see?

Jesus once told the Pharisees, "If you were blind, you would not be guilty" (Jn 9:41). Jesus accuses the Pharisees again and again, especially in Matthew, of being blind. Nicodemus is one of those rare individuals who seems to understand that he does not understand. He knows he is blind and so seeks out Jesus.

35

ALL I'VE EVER DONE

John 4:1-42

Used, broken, betrayed
Wounded and so afraid
Five times degraded
Life, a desolate dream
A desert of hope
On my lonely way
Felt like a runaway
In the sweltering (noon) day
Alone, bucket in hand
(But) thirsting for more
There must be some mistake
Beside the well He waits
Come see the One
Who told me all
I've done
He spoke to me
Could He be
The Chosen One
He set me free
From all my memories
Washed from my sin
Never again
Thirsty no more
Standing there in the heat

> *Thirsty with tired feet*
> *Unexpected greeting*
> *He spoke gentle and calm*
> *"Give me a drink"*
> *How could He not see?*
> *The impropriety to speak to me*
> *Such relentless pursuit*
> *Invincible love*
> *Oh, if only you knew*
> *The One who's asking you*
> *You could have asked me*
> *And I would have granted free*
> *An eternal spring, the offer I bring*
> *The water of life*
> *Will spring up inside*
> *A never-ending tide*
> *The moment you see*
> *That I am He speaking to you*
> Cowritten with Ginny Owens

ALL I'VE EVER DONE

It was a road Jesus frequented. At least three and perhaps four times a year he traveled this road as he made the journey from Galilee to Jerusalem. Sometimes preachers and commentaries say that Jesus' going through Samaria and not around it exhibits some sort of exceptional openness on his part. After all, Jews have nothing to do with Samaritans, the text itself says as much. The truth is, Josephus tells us that Galileans had no misgivings about traveling the road through Samaria.

It is one of the many unique stories of John involving Jesus spending an extended period of time speaking to just one person.

He is there waiting for her at the legendary well Jacob had given to his sons. It's a historic spot, and history is about to be made there again. She wearily shuffles in his direction until she sees him standing there. Gathering herself she prepares for the abuse she's become used to over time, especially from men.

To the contrary, he asks for help, for a drink from the collapsible leather bucket she carries with her to lower into the well. He will reveal himself to her in a minute as the source of the living water that is the Spirit. But for now, he is thirsty. The exchange between the two of them is complicated. He is in loving pursuit. She is throwing sand in his face, trying to get away. But Jesus is relentless.

The Twelve return with provisions from town. John tells us that they are surprised, but not that Jesus is talking to a Samaritan. After all, we know Galileans have no problem speaking to them. They are surprised that he is talking to a woman. Men simply do not speak to women in public, not even their own wives. But they seem to know better than to ask Jesus why.

Jesus had revealed her past, had unpacked the festering wound-edness of her five failed marriages and of the relationship she was currently in with a man who did not love her enough to make her his wife. The people from town had been revealing her past to her for years, condemning, judging, humiliating. But Jesus' revelation was somehow different. There was no condemnation, no judgment, no humiliation. She runs excitedly back into town, having tasted some of that living water Jesus offered. Apparently, Jesus never got his drink.

♫ *LYRIC NOTE* ♫

There is no single lyric to point out in this song. What stands out to the careful listener is a uniquely feminine quality about the music and the lyric. Ginny Owens and I wrote this song together, and she contributed that unique point of view in the gentle poignant music and words.

36

COME to ME and DRINK

John 7:1-44

Violent men were lurking
In amidst the festive crowd
Who'd made a solemn vow
To take His life
But Jesus stood up, unafraid
Of all that they might do
Of angry fists and cruel stones
Of sharp and bloody knives
The Tabernacle Feast had reached
Its last and greatest day
And there was dancing, singing psalms of praise
As they celebrated Moses
And the rock that had been struck
The crowd that filled the Temple court
At last heard Jesus say
　If anyone is thirsty
　Let them come to Me and drink
　The Living Water comes from deep inside
　To everyone who will believe
　An inner spring will flow
　Welling up into Eternal Life

With joy you will draw water

From salvation's well

You will trust and never be afraid

The Lord will be your strength and song

And you will proclaim

And shout out loud and sing for joy

The glory of His name

If you know that you are thirsty

If your heart and soul are dry

And deep within, you're barren as a stone

Then hear His fearless promise

Spoken every day anew

For all who thirst, who are afraid

Lost and all alone

COME TO ME AND DRINK

It may very well be the most dramatic, public moment in the story of Jesus, and we tend to read right past it. Understanding the story demands that we listen closely and over several verses. In John 7:2 we are told it is the Feast of Tabernacles. Thirty-six verses later we are told it is the "last and greatest day of the feast." The background provides the key.

Tabernacles (Sukkoth, Booths) is one of the three great feasts of the Jewish year, the Shalosh Regalim. It is referred to as a "pilgrimage feast" because everyone who lived within a prescribed distance (twenty-five miles) was required to make the pilgrimage to Jerusalem and celebrate within the city walls. What does that mean? The city is absolutely packed! The temple court where Jesus shouts the words of verse 37 is teeming with tens of thousands of people. It is almost certainly his most public pronouncement.

John assumes we know what happens on the last and greatest day of the feast. He assumes we know about the high priest pouring out a pitcher of water, drawn from the pool of Siloam, before the massive crowd that fills the thirty-six-acre temple court. He takes it for granted that we know that the high priest, on the last and greatest day of the feast, stands before the crowd on the porch of the temple and shouts these words: "With joy you will draw water from the wells of salvation!" (Is 12:3; m. Sukkoth 4:1, 9-10).

That is the setting for Jesus' most public pronouncement. He had said as much earlier in John 4 in that extremely private moment with the woman at the well. Now he shouts it to the thousands in response to the words of the high priest: "If anyone is thirsty, let them come to me and drink!"

♫ LYRIC NOTE ♫

With joy you will draw water
From salvation's well
You will trust and never be afraid
The Lord will be your strength and song
And you will proclaim
And shout out loud and sing for joy
The glory of His name

This lyric attempts to put to music a somewhat complex moment from John's Gospel. The setting must be presented as well as the statement of the high priest quoting Isaiah 12, which is not provided in the actual text. This is accomplished by means of a bridge, which is neither a verse nor a chorus and is sung by a different voice. This is almost certainly the most complicated scene from the Gospels I have ever tried to set to music.

37

SCRIBBLING in the SAND

John 8:1-11

Amidst a mob of madmen, she stood frightened and alone
As hate-filled voices hissed at Him that she must now be stoned
But in the air around Him hung a vast and wordless love
Who knows what luminous lesson He was in the middle of?
At first He faced the fury of their self-righteous scorn
But then He stooped and at once became the calm eye of the storm
It was His wordless answer to their dark and cruel demand
A lifetime in a moment as He scribbled in the sand

    It was silence. It was music
    It was art. It was absurd
    He stooped and shouted volumes
    Without saying one single word
    The same finger of the strong hand
    That had written ten commands
    For now was simply scribbling in the sand

Within the space of space and time He'd scribbled in the sand
They came to hear and see as much as they could understand
Now bound by cords of kindness they couldn't cast a single stone
And Jesus and the woman found that they were all alone
Could that same Finger come and trace on my soul's sacred sand
And make some unexpected space where I could understand

> *That my own condemnation pierced and broke that gentle Hand*
> *That scratched the words I'll never know*
> *Written in the sand*
> Music by Phil Naish

SCRIBBLING IN THE SAND

Twice John tells us Jesus knelt down and "wrote down" (*kategraphen*) something with his fingertip in the sacred sand of the temple. So, what did he write? Apparently, John thinks we don't need to know. We have to learn to trust that, given the perfection of the Word of God, John gives us all we need to know. It is an unanswerable question. Not only is it unanswerable, it is the wrong question. (This does not mean that it is still not a good question.)

There is a good chance that John assumes his readers know about Jeremiah 17:13:

> All who abandon you
> will be put to shame.
> All who turn away from me
> will be written in the dirt,
> for they have abandoned
> the LORD, the fountain of living water.

It is a fairly safe assumption that John's readers know this verse. It is a far less safe assumption to think that we, his contemporary readers, know it. But that is not the point. What is absolutely rock solid certain is that the religious leaders who have dragged the woman before Jesus as a trap unquestionably know this verse. That is the point. Not what Jesus wrote but *that he wrote*. It was what the scholars refer to as prophetic activity, an act outside the norm of behavior that calls attention to itself. It prepares the unlistening crowd to hear Jesus' final words: "Let anyone who is without sin cast the first stone."

They are prophetic words as well, uttered by the One who had just reenacted a passage from Jeremiah.

♫ *LYRIC NOTE* ♫

This is as good a place as any to point out the obvious error in this lyric. Jesus definitely did not *scribble* in the sand. He deliberately wrote something down!

38

JESUS WEPT

John 11:1-37

Familiar figure comes
Now He's three days late
How could He take so long?
Why did He hesitate?
Two women question Him
Both weeping as they come
Completely different
And yet they're both the same
Martha's grasping
At some vague religious hope
Endless anxiety
She can barely cope
But Mary's gasping with
Her own hopeful fear
Lazarus would not have died
If you had been here
Did Jesus weep
For their disbelief
Or did He cry
Because His friend had died
Took on Himself
All of their pain and fear

> *Oh the mystery of*
> *His silent tears*
> *He stood beside the tomb*
> *Of His beloved friend*
> *And shouted out those words*
> *They could not comprehend*
> *Then rose the smiling corpse*
> *Familiar silhouette*
> *It was a moment*
> *They never would forget*
> *Jesus wept that day*
> *Mysterious, silent tears*
> *The reason that He cried*
> *It never will be clear*
> *But there's one certain thing*
> *For now that we can say*
> *He had come to wipe*
> *All our tears away*

JESUS WEPT

John was not the only "beloved" disciple. Lazarus is also described as "the one he loved." And now he has died. Jesus' beloved friend is dead. He had received word of Lazarus's fatal illness in plenty of time to come and heal him before he died. Yet Jesus stayed where he was for three costly days. It's almost as if he wanted his friend to die. He let it happen! The text leaves us with no choice but to wonder why.

Martha and Mary are wondering as well. Martha with her head and Mary with her heart. They greet Jesus with precisely the same words, but coming from the two of them, as different as they were, those words have a completely different meaning. Jesus engages Martha with a discussion about his true nature. He simply weeps with Mary, is "deeply moved."

On the way out of town to the tomb "Jesus wept" (the shortest verse in the Bible). On the way, he weeps. And we are left to wonder about just one more thing. The crowd believes he is weeping because of how much he loved Lazarus. But if you've been listening closely to the Gospel of John, you've learned that the crowd is almost always wrong. There must be another reason, and John chooses not to engage the obvious question.

So often we want the answer to be one thing, but rarely in such complicated emotional moments are things that simple. Perhaps there were several reasons for Jesus' tears. Perhaps he was frustrated, angry at death itself and all it has robbed from his friend. Maybe he was just so tired that seeing the others weeping, especially Mary, with whom he has a special emotional connection, he simply could not hold back the tears. Perhaps he is contemplating what is waiting for him in Jerusalem in just a few days. After all, it will include a tomb and mourners, many of these same mourners in fact. Perhaps he is weeping for their disbelief in his ability to do anything now that Lazarus is dead. Or just maybe it is a bit of all these things.

♫ LYRIC NOTE ♫

One certain thing
That we can say
He had come to wipe
All their tears away

The chorus poses various questions as to why Jesus might have wept at the tomb of Lazarus. The lyric leaves those questions unanswered. The final line of the song states what really matters. It is not the unanswerable question, it is the certainty that Jesus has promised to wipe all our tears away.

39

ONE LONG FINAL WALK

John 14–17

The moment has come, now we must go

The battle's begun, the full moon's aglow

One final meal, one final talk

One long final walk

I am the Vine, the One who is true

Remain in Me, My Word is in you

You are the branches, speaking the Truth

And bearing the fruit

Now love one another

As I have loved you

This is My command

That your joy will be full

As the world's hated Me, so it will hate you

For the work I have done no one else could do

The Word I have spoken, all who refuse

Will have no excuse

When the Comforter comes, I'll send Him to you

He will testify, the Spirit of Truth

Who comes from the Father to live in your hearts

For You were there from the start

I have more to say

> *That you cannot hear*
> *When the Comforter comes*
> *Everything will be clear*
> *The hour has come, you'll flee in fear*
> *But I am not alone, My Father is here*
> *So don't be afraid and trust in My Word*
> *I've conquered the world*
> Music by Scott Brasher

ONE LONG FINAL WALK

Both Matthew and Mark tell us that immediately after Peter's statement, "Even if everyone else deserts you, I never will," they left the upper room and made their way to the garden. John gives no specifics. What he does provide at this point in the narrative is four solid chapters of Jesus' final words to the disciples, the longest uninterrupted discourse we have. I like to imagine that it didn't take place at the table after the meal because, after all, they have no time to dawdle. I imagine this longest talk taking place on the long final walk to the garden.

It is hardly more than a mile from inside the old city of Jerusalem to one of the gates on the eastern side of the city, across the Kidron Valley to Gethsemane. I hear these words spoken along that path. They feel like the kind of discourse that would occur peripatetically, that is, on a walk.

They are his final words in a sense. His concluding words of his earthly ministry. His final words before the arrest, crucifixion, and resurrection. He must have chosen them with special care, though there is every indication the Eleven were not listening very closely. Too much is swirling around them. Too many disturbing things have been said. But Jesus tells them in John 14:25-26 that when the Spirit is given, they will remember and understand them.

The question to ask then is, what seems to be on his mind as Jesus walks this final walk with the Eleven? What are these most significant words he wants to leave with them? One of the best ways to determine this is to listen for repetition, for repeated words and themes.

The two words that recur more than any others are *remain* (twelve times) and *love* (thirteen times). (His later prayer in John 17 is dominated by the word *glory*.)

Remain in me and I will *remain* in you (Jn 15:4). If you *remain* in me and my words *remain* in you . . . (Jn 15:7). As the Father has *loved* me, so have I *loved* you (Jn 15:9). *Remain* in my *love* (Jn 15:10). *Love* each other as I have *loved* you (Jn 15:12). This is my command: *love* each other (Jn 15:17).

What seems especially heavy on Jesus' heart and mind is that his disciples do not stray, wander, or abandon his teaching. That is, he wants them to *remain*, to stay, to abide, to resist the temptation to stray. And the glue that will hold them to his Word and to each other is *love*.

♪ *LYRIC NOTE* ♪

This wonderful melody from Scott Brasher reminded me of a walk when he first played it. There is a steady rhythm to it, almost like footsteps. Once that was clear, it was simply a matter of working through the teaching of Jesus in chapters 14–18.

40

STRANGER on
the SHORE

John 21

In the early morning mist they saw a stranger on the seashore
He somehow seemed familiar, asking what the night had brought
With taut anticipation then they listened to his orders
And pulling in the net found more than they had ever caught
The one he loved first recognized the stranger there was Jesus
He alone remembered this had happened once before
The one who had denied him, who had once walked on the water
Jumped in and swam to him to be confronted on the shore
  You need to be confronted by the stranger on the shore
  You need to have him search your soul; you need to hear the call
  You need to learn exactly what it means for you to follow
  You need to realize that he's asking for it all
The meal he had prepared for them was waiting on the fire
The smell of bread, the sizzle of the fish upon the coals
The laughter and the joy at once more being all together
They didn't realize that he was searching all their souls
Then came the painful questions that would pierce the soul of Simon
A threefold chance to reaffirm the love he had denied
The gentle eyes that saw his heart and waited for an answer
Had seen the look upon my face the moment he had lied

You need to be confronted by the stranger on the shore
You need to have him search your soul; you need to hear the call
You need to learn exactly what it means for you to follow
You need to realize that he's asking for it all

STRANGER ON THE SHORE

If you listen closely to John's Gospel, you will hear a conclusion at the end of chapter 20. Verse 31 pretty well sums up the entire book. But then the text takes off again with chapter 21. Language experts note that the tone and vocabulary shift with the chapter break. Figures of speech occur that haven't happened anywhere else in the Gospel (e.g., "it happened this way . . ."). John 21 represents another voice altogether. While the voice may have changed, the content is still John's. The account of the second miraculous catch is his own eyewitness testimony. So why does any of this matter? I believe it is important because it shows how much John's followers love this story. They had heard him tell it countless times. Now he is gone and they tell it to us on his behalf. It is a story that is told nowhere else in any of the Gospels. Only John tells us of the encounter with the Stranger on the seashore.

The day is just dawning and John and the others have fished all night and caught nothing. Jesus has been strangely unrecognizable in many of his postresurrection appearances. Sometimes we are told they "were kept from recognizing him." Perhaps it is because there were no expectations of ever seeing him alive again. Perhaps he is simply too far away (one hundred yards). Perhaps one of those beautiful Galilean sunrises is happening behind him and they only see his silhouette. Apparently, the writer thinks we don't need to know why he was unrecognizable.

There is tension and playfulness in the story. Jesus asks the pointed question, "You haven't caught any fish, have you?" And what must have been their grumbling response. And then a few moments later an explosion of excitement, of flapping fish, of their exclamations, of recognizing it really is Jesus standing on the shore.

He has made breakfast already. Already caught and cleaned fish and made bread. There is absolutely no reason not to believe he did this for them practically every morning. Then there is the walk, Jesus and Peter, with John following like a puppy. There are the three questions that are often misunderstood. Jesus is not humiliating Peter; he is reinstating him to his place of leadership. He renews Peter via confrontation. The questions force Peter to come to the point of the rock-hard confession, "You know everything; you know that I love you."

And this is still Jesus' way: confrontation and renewal. Those questions are meant for you and me as much as they were for Peter. There is not simply one single question. If that were so we might answer and simply move on. But Jesus doesn't want us to move on. There might have been only two questions—the first and then a single follow-up for effect. We might escape two questions. But then there is the third. It leaves us with no place to hide. We sense what Jesus is saying right into our souls with that third question. We are forced to confess that if we were lying, he would know. After all, he knows everything.

So right now, in the sacrament of this present moment, hear Jesus ask you once . . . twice . . . and finally that third inescapable time, "Do you truly love me?"

You need to be confronted by the stranger on the seashore

The first line of the chorus is the key to the lyric of the song. It makes the point that what happened to Peter in John's Gospel must eventually happen to each one of his followers.

CONCLUSION

A Lyrical Life

PHYSICS TEACHES US that when something is struck it resonates, whether it is a string or a drum or a bell. Even empty spaces
have their own unique resonant frequencies. You've experienced it
singing in empty stairways when one note jumps out, noticeably
louder. You've hit on the resonate frequency of that particular spot
on the stairs! (It happens sometimes in the shower too!) It is a fas-
cinating fact and a remarkable metaphor.

Jesus was struck and his life resonated with a song that has been
sung by billions for thousands of years. There are the magnificently
gifted singers, the Bachs and Handels, and there are the children
singing "Jesus loves me this I know." So unutterably magnificent is
Jesus' life that, no matter the skill level of the songwriter or the
singer, or the sophistication of the song itself, what matters most,
the only thing that matters, is him.

Songs have been resonating from Jesus' life as early as AD 52.
That is about the time Paul sang the earliest hymn we know of:

Who, existing in the form of God,

Did not consider equality with God

As something to be exploited. (Phil 2:6)

Isaiah sang about him in the eighth century BC. David in the
tenth century. Luke celebrates the fact that upon hearing that Jesus

was to be born, everyone started singing: Mary, Simeon, the angels. And there is a straight line from them to you and me. We are left, as they were, with that lyrical life of his. That life that, above all else, is so worth listening to and singing about.

Appendix

A MUSICAL OVERVIEW OF THE BIBLE

THE HEBREW BIBLE		
SCRIPTURE	SONG	ALBUM
Genesis 1	Older Than the Rain	The Hidden Face of God
Genesis 1–3	The Beginning	The Beginning
Genesis 11–8	El Shaddai	The Early Works
Genesis 21	They Called Him Laughter	The Beginning
Genesis 22	God Will Provide a Lamb	The Beginning
Genesis 28:32	Asleep on Holy Ground	The Beginning
Exodus 3:7	In the Wilderness	The Beginning
Exodus 34:29	A Face That Shone	The Beginning
Leviticus 25	Jubilee	The Beginning
Numbers 6:24	Barocha	The Beginning
Numbers 24:4-9	Lift Up the Suffering Symbol	The Beginning
Deuteronomy 6	Meditation 3, Shema	The Beginning
Deuteronomy 30:4	The Word Is So Near	The Beginning
Job	Job Suite	The Way of Wisdom
Job 13:24	The Hidden Face of God	The Hidden Face of God
Psalm 13	How Long?	The Way of Wisdom
Psalm 22; 69	The Death of a Son	The Way of Wisdom
Psalm 23	My Shepherd	The Way of Wisdom
Psalm 51	Come Lift Up Your Sorrows	The Hidden Face of God
Psalm 121	My Help	The Way of Wisdom
Psalm 121:1	For F.F.B.	Poiema
Psalm 139	Search Me and Know Me	The Way of Wisdom
Proverbs	The Way of Wisdom	The Way of Wisdom
Ecclesiastes	Under the Sun	The Way of Wisdom
Song of Solomon	Arise My Love	The Way of Wisdom
	Earthly Perfect Harmony	Poiema
The Prophets	The Prophets	The Word
	The Kingdom	The Word

Isaiah 6:11	And a Little Child Shall Lead Them	The Word
Isaiah 7:14	The Promise	The Final Word
Isaiah 7:14	Immanuel	The Final Word
Isaiah 8:14	Scandalon	Scandalon
Isaiah 28:23; 51:4	Will You Not Listen?	The Word
Isaiah 53:5	I Will Not Walk Away from You	The Hidden Face of God
Ezekiel	Then They Will Know	The Word
Ezekiel 14:5	Recapture Me	The Word
Ezekiel 37:1-10	Valley of Dry Bones	The Word
Hosea 1–3	Song of Gomer	The Word
Amos 8:11	So Many Books	The Word
Zephaniah 3:20	I Will Bring You Home	The Word
Malachi 3:2	Who Can Abide?	The Word

THE GOSPELS
BY THEME

THEME	SONG	ALBUM
The Incarnation	To the Mystery	The Final Word
	The Final Word	The Final Word
	His Humanity	Matthew
	The One Who Was Sent	John
	The Bread, the Light . . .	John
	The Light of the World	The Early Works
The Nativity	What Sort of Song?	Luke
	A King in a Cattle Trough	Luke
	Celebrate the Child	The Final Word
	Vicit Agnus Noster	The Promise
	Immanuel	The Final Word
	Spirit of the Age	The Final Word
	And Dreamed	Matthew
	A Simple House	Matthew
Baptism of Jesus	Meditation/Baptism	Scandalon
	Simeon's Song	Luke
	When Jesus Was a Boy	Close Your Eyes . . .
Wedding at Cana	The Wedding	Scandalon
Beatitudes	This Is Who You Are	Matthew
Ministry	The Nazarene	Scandalon
	How Can These Things Be?	John

	The Things We Leave Behind	Poiema
	Come and See	John
	A World Turned Upside Down	Luke
	The Stranger	Mark
	Talitha Koumi	Close Your Eyes . . .
	Let the Children Come	Close Your Eyes . . .
	Scribbling in the Sand	John
	The Bridge	Luke
	The Gentle Healer	Scandalon
	All I've Ever Done	John
	Come to Me and Drink	John
	The Gift to Believe	Matthew
	When Did We See You?	Matthew
	A Breath of a Prayer	Luke
	Go Find Out What This Means	Matthew
	The Kingdom	Matthew
	The Service of the Sod	Mark
	At His Feet	Mark
	You Walk in Lonely Places	Mark
	Jesus Wept	John
	In His Arms	Mark
	The Paradigm	Mark
Storm on the Sea	A Great Wind, a Great Calm . . .	Mark
Triumphal Entry	Ride on to Die	Known by the Scars
	Hosanna	Close Your Eyes . . .
Mary Washes His Feet	In Memory of Her Love	Mark
Last Supper	Come to the Table	Known by the Scars
	How Much More a Servant . . .	Luke
	Basin and the Towel	Poiema
Jesus in the Garden	In the Garden	Known by the Scars
	We Are Not Scattered Strangers	Hidden Face of God
	One Long Final Walk	John
Betrayal of Judas	Traitor's Look	Known by the Scars
The Cross	Why	Known by the Scars
	God Will Provide a Lamb	Legacy
	This Must Be the Lamb	The Early Works
	Cross of Glory	Known by the Scars
	Crown Him	Known by the Scars
	Is It All Over Now?	Mark

Resurrection	The Pain and Persistence of Doubt	Luke
	Seven Endless Miles	Luke
	Love Crucified Arose	The Early Works
	Known by the Scars	Joy in the Journey
Second Miraculous Catch	Stranger on the Shore	A Fragile Stone, John

BY REFERENCE

SCRIPTURE	SONG	ALBUM
Matthew 4:19	Sea of Souls	A Fragile Stone
Matthew 5:1-12	This Is Who You Are	Matthew
Matthew 9:13; 12:8	Go Find Out What This Means	Matthew
Matthew 14:22ff.	Walking on the Water	A Fragile Stone
Matthew 16:18; John 1:42	A Fragile Stone	A Fragile Stone
Matthew 19:14	Let the Children Come	Close Your Eyes . . .
Matthew 19:16ff.; Mark 2	What Will It Take to Keep You from Jesus?	Scandalon
Matthew 21:9; Mark 11:9 John 12:13	Hosanna	Close Your Eyes
Mark 1:1	The Beginning	Mark
Mark 3:21ff.	God's Own Fool	Scandalon
Mark 4:1-35	The Service of the Sod	Mark
Mark 4:35-41	A Great Wind, a Great Calm	Mark
Mark 5	At His Feet	Mark
Mark 5:41	Talitha Koumi	Close Your Eyes . . .
Mark 6:27-31	You Walk in Lonely Places	Mark
Mark 8:27ff.	Not That Kind of King	A Fragile Stone
Mark 9:33-37; 10:13-16	In His Arms	Mark
Mark 10:28	I Left Everything to Follow You	A Fragile Stone
Mark 10:46-52	The Paradigm	Mark
Mark 14:1-9	In Memory of Her Love	Mark
Mark 16:3-8	Is It All Over Now?	Mark
Luke 1:26-55	What Sort of Song?	Luke
Luke 2:1-20	A King in a Cattle Trough	Luke
Luke 2:25-35	Simeon's Song	Luke
Luke 2:41-52	A Little Boy Lost	Luke
Luke 2:41-52	When Jesus Was a Boy	Close Your Eyes

Luke 6:17-26	A World Turned Upside Down	Luke
Luke 10:25-37	The Bridge	Luke
Luke 11:1-4	A Breath of a Prayer	Luke
Luke 22:14-30	How Much More a Servant . . .	Luke
Luke 22:61 (John 1:42)	His Gaze	A Fragile Stone
Luke 24:1-12	The Pain and Persistence . . .	Luke
Luke 24:13-35	Seven Endless Miles	Luke
John 1:39	Come and See	John
John 2:12ff.	The Lamb Is a Lion	Scandalon
John 3:1-13	How Can These Things Be?	John
John 4:1-42	All I've Ever Done	John
John 5:24, 38	The One Who Was Sent	John
John 6:35; 8:12; 11:25	The Bread, the Light, the Life	John
John 7:1-44	Come to Me and Drink	John
John 8	Scribbling in the Sand	John
John 11:35	Jesus Wept	John
John 6:35; 8:12; 11:25	The Bread, the Light, the Life	John
John 13:4	The Basin and the Towel	Poiema
John 15–16	One Long Final Walk	John
John 21	Stranger on the Shore	A Fragile Stone, John

ACTS, EPISTLES, AND REVELATION

SCRIPTURE	SONG	ALBUM
Acts 10:9ff. (John 21:18)	I'm Not Supposed to Be Here	A Fragile Stone
Acts 12:17	Mourning the Death of a Dream	A Fragile Stone
Romans 12:5	Flesh of His Flesh	Present Reality
1 Corinthians 1:19-25	Could It Be?	Present Reality
1 Corinthians 10:13	The Edge	Poiema
1 Corinthians 11:23ff.	Meditation 2/Eucharist	Present Reality
2 Corinthians 8:9	Distressing Disguise	Present Reality
Galatians 3; Romans 3:22	That's What Faith Must Be	Present Reality
Ephesians 1:9	Live This Mystery	Present Reality
Ephesians 2:10	The Poem of Your Life	Poiema
Philippians 2:6-11	Carmen Christi	The Final Word

Philippians 3:10	Know You in the Now	Present Reality
Colossians 3:15	In Stillness and Simplicity	Present Reality
Colossians 3:16	The Word	Present Reality
1 Thessalonians 4:13	Maranatha	Known by the Scars
1 Thessalonians 5:8	Hope	Poiema
Hebrews 3:6; 6:19	Soul Anchor	Soul Anchor
Hebrews 4:9	Seventh Sunrise	Soul Anchor
Hebrews 5:8; 13:3	A Violent Grace	Soul Anchor
Hebrews 6:9	Hope	Poiema
Hebrews 5:7	He Was Heard	Known by the Scars
Hebrews 9:28	He Was Heard	Soul Anchor
Hebrews 10:20	A New and Living Way	Soul Anchor
Hebrews 10:33; 12:2	Fellow Prisoners	Soul Anchor
Hebrews 11; 12:1-3	By Faith	Soul Anchor
Hebrews 11:13	Pilgrims to the City of God	Soul Anchor
Hebrews 13:1, 4, 8, 13, 25	Grace Be With You All	Soul Anchor
Hebrews 13:5	Never Will I Leave You	Soul Anchor
1 Peter 2:4	Living Stones	A Fragile Stone
Revelation 1	The Unveiling	Unveiled Hope
Revelation 2–3	To the Overcomers	Unveiled Hope
Revelation 4:8	Holy, Holy, Holy	Unveiled Hope
Revelation 4:11; 5:9-13	You Are Worthy	Unveiled Hope
Revelation 7:10-17	Salvation	Unveiled Hope
Revelation 12–13	The Dragon	Unveiled Hope
Revelation 15:3ff.	The Song of the Lamb	Unveiled Hope
Revelation 18	The City of Doom	Unveiled Hope
Revelation 19	Hallelujah	Unveiled Hope
Revelation 21	The New Jerusalem	Unveiled Hope

LYRIC AND MUSIC CREDITS

All lyrics and music associated with *The Nazarene* were written by Michael Card with the following exceptions:

Chapter 6	"His Humanity," music by Scott Brasher
Chapter 7	"The Gift to Believe," cowritten with Scott Roley
Chapter 8	"When Did We See You?" cowritten with Scott Roley
Chapter 10	"The Kingdom," music by Scott Brasher
Chapter 12	"A Great Wind, a Great Calm, a Great Fear," cowritten with Sarah Hart
Chapter 14	"The Stranger," cowritten with Chuck Beckman
Chapter 15	"At His Feet," music by Scott Brasher
Chapter 16	"You Walk in Lonely Places," cowritten with Sarah Hart
Chapter 19	"In Memory of Her Love," cowritten with Sarah Hart
Chapter 20	"Is It All Over Now?" cowritten with Brown Bannister
Chapter 21	"A World Turned Upside Down," cowritten with Scott Brasher and Joan Brasher
Chapter 27	"A Breath of a Prayer," cowritten with Scott Roley
Chapter 28	"How Much More a Servant Could He Be?" cowritten with Scott Roley
Chapter 29	"The Pain and Persistence of Doubt," music by Scott Brasher
Chapter 31	"Come and See," cowritten with Jon Reddick
Chapter 33	"The One Who Was Sent," cowritten with Scott Roley
Chapter 35	"All I've Ever Done," cowritten with Ginny Owens
Chapter 37	"Scribbling in the Sand," music by Phil Naish
Chapter 39	"One Long Final Walk," music by Scott Brasher

ABOUT THE AUTHOR

For many years Michael Card has struggled to listen to Scripture at the level of the imagination. The result has been thirty-seven albums and twenty-seven books, all examining a different element of the Bible, from the life of the apostle Peter to slavery in the New Testament to Christ-centered creativity.

He has a master's degree in biblical studies from Western Kentucky University as well as honorary PhDs in music (Whitfield Seminary) and Christian education (Philadelphia Biblical University).

He lives with his wife, Susan, and their four children in Franklin, Tennessee, where together they pursue racial reconciliation and neighborhood renewal.

WWW.MICHAELCARD.COM

Also Available from
MICHAEL CARD

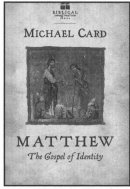

**Matthew: The Gospel
of Identity**

978-0-8308-3772-4

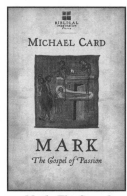

**Mark: The Gospel
of Passion**

978-0-8308-7818-5

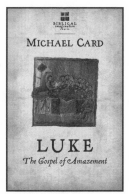

**Luke: The Gospel
of Amazement**

978-0-8308-3254-5

**John: The Gospel
of Wisdom**

978-0-8308-3445-7

Inexpressible
A Fragile Stone: The Emotional Life of Simon Peter
Scribbling in the Sand: Christ and Creativity
A Violent Grace: Meeting Christ at the Cross